The Dark Path

The Dark Path

A Memoir

DAVID SCHICKLER

RIVERHEAD BOOKS   *a member of Penguin Group (USA) New York 2013*

RIVERHEAD BOOKS
Published by the Penguin Group
Penguin Group (USA), 375 Hudson Street,
New York, New York 10014, USA

USA · Canada · UK · Ireland · Australia
New Zealand · India · South Africa · China

Penguin Books Ltd, Registered Offices: 80 Strand, London WC2R 0RL, England
For more information about the Penguin Group visit penguin.com

ISBN 978-1-59448-645-6

Printed in the United States of America
1   3   5   7   9   10   8   6   4   2

Book design by Gretchen Achilles

*Penguin is committed to publishing works of quality and integrity.
In that spirit, we are proud to offer this book to our readers;
however, the story, the experiences, and the words
are the author's alone.*

Author's Note

I changed the names, places of origin, and identifying characteristics of many people in this memoir to honor their privacy, and I was tempted to make them all seven-foot-tall Canadian podiatrists raised by wolves. That way I could have pretended that they were merely colorful fictions.

But they aren't fictions. Everyone in this story was and is real. Whether I got punched by him, or slept with her, each person acted nearly just as I've written. This is a work of memory, though, so here come the caveats: a lover who shouts may have whispered . . . a slapped face may have been a shoved shoulder. I compressed time sparingly.

The truth still comes through, I believe. The bullies were bullies, that wild girl was wild, the gentle were gentle. I'm still discerning whether I was wild, gentle, both, or neither. In the meantime, I hope all the people in this story are still out there being their truest selves, thriving somehow, with grace on their side. I hope we all are.

For John Francis Schickler
and Luke Francis Schickler

For Martha Alison Schickler
and Cora Alison Schickler

For Peggy Schickler

And for Larry Wroblewski, S.J.,
my first and best writing teacher
and a wonderful priest

This nearness to you in the darkness is too simple and too close for excitement. It is commonplace for all things to live an unexpected life in the night.

—THOMAS MERTON

The Dark Path

Chapter One

I'M TEN YEARS OLD, sitting at Mass, listening to my sweet wife cry while I watch the priest. My wife is Caitlin Brenner, the blond, blue-eyed beauty who is snuffling quietly in the pew three back from mine, and the priest is Father Jonas, who's up on the altar blessing the Eucharist on this Easter morning, 1980. I look back at weepy Caitlin and then I look again at Father Jonas, like I'm supposed to, like we're all supposed to. I'm caught between them.

Caitlin hasn't agreed to marry me yet. We rarely talk, but soon she'll realize that we each have four syllables total in our names and both our last names end with -er. David Schickler. Caitlin Brenner. This means that we shall wed and have four children. Caitlin and I are the best spellers in the Saint Helen's parish fifth-grade class. She came in second in the spelling bee last month by spelling *penniless*. I beat her by spelling *seismograph*, and when Caitlin heard me do so, she probably wanted to make out with me right then to congratulate me, I'm convinced of it, even though all she did in actuality was look pissed off and then mock my upside-down brown bowl of a haircut.

Now, here at Mass, three pews back with her family, Caitlin is crying because her old, smeary-eyed cocker spaniel, Gus, died last week. She's been weeping about him at school, too. I've wanted to comfort her with apples, as the Bible says, which would be easy since this is Rochester, in upstate New York, apple country. But I haven't said anything to her, and even just being a few feet away from her is making my blood jump.

"May the body of Christ bring you everlasting life," booms Father Jonas from the altar.

He makes my blood jump, too. Not romantically, the way Caitlin does, but spiritually and deeply anyway. He's powerful because he's a priest, but he's also just cool. Father Jonas is young, with jet-black hair and a tan. Down in Brazil he runs a mission school for boys and each spring he visits our parish to ask for donations. Even Tommy Marzipretta, a mustachioed bully of a boy in our congregation, shuts up when Father Jonas speaks. The man has an edge. As I watch him raise the wafer, a deep part of me says, *Be like him, David. Have that edge. Spend your life consecrating the host, turning something plain into God. Be a priest.*

Caitlin sniffles more loudly. I turn and try to use telepathy on her. I use telepathy when I'm afraid of talking. *Don't worry, Caitlin,* I tell her with my eyes. *The Book of Revelation says that God will wipe away your every tear, but how about if instead— surprise!—it's me, Dave Schickler, who wipes your tears away? I want to skate with you at Olympic Roller Rink, and your eyes are the bluest answers to all of life's questions and—*

"David? What are you staring at?"

It's my father, sitting beside me. His name is John but the world calls him Jack. Beyond him are my three sisters and my mother.

I'm still focused on Caitlin, bombarding her with woo.

"David," my father says, "turn around and sit still. Enough rumpus."

Every Sunday the six of us sit three rows back from the front on the right side of the church's main aisle. That's the Schickler row.

"Rumpus," says my younger sister, Jeanne, trying out the word. She is six.

My two elder sisters, Anne Marie and Pamela, have their heads together. They're whispering the lyrics to Kool and the Gang's "Ladies Night" and using their fingers on their palms to go over choreography for an upcoming dance recital. All my sisters dance constantly, *ballet-jazz-tap, step-ball-change, pas de bourrée.*

Anne Marie and Pamela start doing sexy growls like Kool himself. My mother, Peggy, sighs and my sisters' chatter stops.

During Mass my mother closes her eyes and travels to somewhere deep and private.

"Pay attention, David," says my father.

I try, but it's Easter and the colors in church are extra wrong. Mrs. Millichek, the acoustic guitarist, is wearing an alarmingly yellow dress. She is so yellow, I can't pray. Many other parishioners are wearing outfits with Easter-eggy colors—orange, yellow, pink, lavender. These colors are making me headachy and nauseous. Now it's time to go up for Communion, but here comes Mr. Bonticello, the usher, wearing the same robin's-egg-blue suit that he always does each Sunday, and his suit is making me itch because the color is too weak and too lame to have anything to do with God.

"David," says my father. "Communion time."

I don't move. I focus on the hat hooks on the back of the pew before me. I love these hooks. They're made of heavy brass and they feel strong and necessary under my thumb. They're the opposite of Mr. Bonticello's suit.

"What's the matter?" asks my father.

I want to tell him, *That guy's suit is messing with me. That suit sucks.*

My father pats my shoulder. "The air's just close in here, buddy. We'll be out soon."

I follow him up to the priest. When I swallow the wafer, I wait for God to bloom to life in my stomach, to give me muscles or wisdom. God doesn't seem to do this, but I'm hoping that one day He will.

After Communion my father lets me go to the back foyer while he and my mother and sisters stay for the final hymn. As I often do when I'm alone in the foyer, I visit the stand of white votive candles. Each is contained in a bloodred stained-glass holder. These lit candles are like secrets that call out to me. They are so beautiful—the strong clean whiteness of them against the deep red stained glass!—that I need to take part in them somehow. I feel this strange urge each Sunday, and the urge seems better obeyed than understood. So I plunge my fingers into the warm, white, waxy meat below the wicks, until all my fingers are coated and dripping.

"Schickler, you retarded faggot, what the hell are you doing?"

I turn, surprised, my face flushing. Tommy Marzipretta stands a few feet away, scowling. Tommy lives in a neighborhood near mine. He is two years older than I am and he goes to public school and likes to punch people. I was in his house once and his parents have a Dallas Cowboys cheerleaders poster taped on the ceiling over their bed and on their nightstand was the book *Jaws*. On my parents' nightstand are copies of the Catholic magazine *Commonweal* and several rosaries, those snakes made of beads, coiled and holy and slithering everywhere.

Standing with Tommy now in the church foyer is his nine-year-old brother, Tony.

I look at the wax on my fingers. "I . . . like these candles."

Tommy shakes his head. "You're a tard, Schickler."

Tony laughs and nudges Tommy. "How come he's such a tard?"

"Who knows?" Tommy shrugs. "Tards are tards. They do tard things."

The congregation lets out, sweeping the Marzipretta boys away and my father to my side. I look at him, relieved. He's six feet tall, with black hair and black, serious eyes. He's an executive for General Motors at their Rochester Products Division, but he grew up on a farm and has country-strong shoulders. I look more like my mother—my green eyes are knockoffs of her blue ones—and although my shoulders are tough like my father's, they'll never be quite as tough as his, as all of him. I once saw two-by-fours fall from our garage rafters onto his head and he just glared at them.

He sees the wax on my fingers and sighs. "Again?" he says.

My family and I drive home to Twin Circle Drive, the cul-de-sac we live on. Once I'm inside I change into jeans and a sweatshirt. My sisters are in the living room, working on their Kool and the Gang routine. They are always working on dance routines. I know the steps and they ask me to join in, but right now I need the path, so I beg off and put on my coat and boots and head outside.

Twin Circle Drive borders a woods and on the other side of the woods is Black Creek Country Club golf course, a private club to which my family partially belongs (we don't have the money to be full, golfing members, but we're social members, meaning we can eat in the club and swim in the pool). Our back lawn blends into the Black Creek woods as seamlessly as the inside of a wardrobe becoming Narnia.

The Black Creek clubhouse, grand like an English country estate, is just half a mile from Twin Circle Drive, but the woods between them are vast. There is a path—just dirt in most places, paved in a few—that cuts from my backyard through these woods, then cuts down a hill, then skirts between the forest and the tenth-hole pond, and finally ends behind the club greenskeeper's garage. Almost every day for almost as long as I can remember, I've walked this path.

It is a dark path. The huge cherry, oak, and maple trees that crowd the woods and loom over the path keep it shaded year-round. The nearby tenth-hole pond always seems to have blue twilight hanging over it, every minute of every day of the year.

On this Easter morning I walk to a spot on the path—my spot—where I stand on the narrow strip of land between the woods and pond. I face the woods and stare at the low pockets of shadows among the trees. I trust these shadows. Like the brass hat hooks and the white candle wax at church, these shadows call to me. They feel like they were put on earth so that I wouldn't miss out on something special. But I trust the shadows more than the hat hooks and wax because the shadows are alive, and they're close to my home, and they're less public, more secret. On summer nights they come alive with green ticking sounds. Possibly they contain hobbits. Even when the woods are snowy, these shadows are here, black, serene, and deep.

I stand on the path now and stare at the shadows and then I do what I always do alone here and that I so often can't do in church. I pray.

Dear Lord, I pray. *Please help me to stop being a retarded faggot. I know that words like* retarded *and* faggot *might offend You, but I have to use them sometimes, Lord. If I don't occasionally call other kids in my class tards, then I myself will be called a tard. I'm sorry, but it's true. Help me to stop shoving my fingers into candles and to stop crying whenever I hear that song "Shining Star" by The Manhattans. I don't want to cry, but then I hear "Shining Star" and it's beautiful. Candle-shoving and crying at songs are tard things for a boy to do, so help me to stop. Amen, Lord. Okay, now You go. You talk.*

I wait for the darkness to speak. I don't expect God to talk to me out loud right this second, but I believe that on some crucial day He will. I know my Bible and God pretty much lets people hear His Voice only once per lifetime. It's usually a blunt plan for the rest of your existence: *This is what you are to say to the Israelites . . . I AM has sent me to you.* Or, *Pick up your mat and walk!*

I listen for my marching orders. I know that somehow, when God talks to me, He will do it from the shadows, from the dark path.

I talk to no one about this, but I walk on the path often. I keep an eye out for Frodo Baggins and an ear out for God.

IT'S JULY, three months later, and I'm at the country club pool and Lesley Hendrik is wearing a navy blue two-piece bathing suit. Lesley is my age and lives on Raven Road, just across the golf course from Twin Circle Drive. Raven Road is also where Tommy Marzipretta lives, so I steer clear of that neighborhood. But thankfully the Hendriks belong to the club and the Marziprettas don't. I love it when Lesley shows up at the pool. She has amber eyes and long, syrup-brown hair which she ties back in a braid when she swims. She has a four-syllable name. Lesley is my summer wife, though I've never told her. She is special because her family is of Dutch descent (unheard of in our mostly Italian corner of Rochester), and she's dangerous because she's a Protestant.

I'm underwater right now, holding my breath, trying to outlast my best friend and next-door neighbor, Scott Barella, who's underwater beside me. He's holding his nose and his face is about to explode with laughter. To make sure that I don't laugh, I'm looking away from Scott, toward the deep end, where Lesley and my elder sisters and other girls are practicing the loveliest thing ever, girls' water ballet. They're gearing up for the club's end-of-summer show. I watch Lesley scissor-kick until my lungs ache, and then I surface.

"You beat me by twenty seconds," says Scott. "Minghia!"

"Minghia" (pronounced MEEN-gyah) is a saying that rules the neighborhoods of Twin Circle Drive and Raven Road. It comes from an Italian word for *dick*, and it basically means "Holy shit!" or "Fucking A!" If I say it in my German-Irish household and my father hears, I get chores.

Scott and I climb out of the pool. From the vending machines we get Sunkist sodas and Snickers bars and sit on the grass near the tenth-hole tee to watch golfers. After our snack we walk home on the dark path, and Scott knows to let me get past my favorite spot in silence. Sometimes we stray into the woods on our way home. We dig giant foxholes to play War and find broken china plates buried in the dirt. On this evening, though, we stay on the path and Scott invites me over for dinner.

"I can't come," I say. "We're having Father Anselm over."

"Shit bomb." Scott says this when he's bummed or surprised.

Father Anselm is our pastor at Saint Helen's. He is tall with thick white hair and he's too cheerful. At dinner my mother serves him roast beef and Blue Nun wine. I sit between the priest and my dad. Father Anselm tousles my hair and talks about the upcoming parish Country Fair.

"You gonna win some goldfish, sport?" he asks me. His laugh is a cluck. "Or a nifty stuffed panda?"

Nifty, I think, and I get my headachy, nauseous feeling. It happens when I'm around God people, priests or nuns, and they talk all bubbly-safe, meaning all chipper and scrubbed too clean. I can't help that it happens. It's like Mr. Bonticello in his pastel-colored suit in church. It freaks me out. It's wrong.

"David," says my mother, "eat your mashed potatoes. You love them."

"Say," clucks Father Anselm, "did you see that AC unit Skip Gibson donated for the raffle? It's a dilly!"

I look at the priest. *Don't say "nifty,"* I command him with telepathy. *Don't say "dilly."*

My father leans toward me. "What's the matter?"

I look at him and think, *This guy is talking wrong. He is too bubbly-safe. He's not telling the truth.*

"Nothing," I say. I take a bite of mashed potatoes.

ON A HOT August night a month later, I go to the girls' water ballet show at the club pool. I sit in a folding chair near the rest of the audience. Our chairs are set up around the pool, a ways back from the water's edge. Stars are wheeling in the night sky and there's a breeze pushing around the branches of the three-story pine trees that ring the pool. Underwater lights are making the pool glow blue.

Twenty girls line up and strike poses along the deep-end edge for the opening number. Barry Manilow's "Could It Be Magic" comes over the speakers and lights spangle off the girls' matching black and silver swimsuits. Lesley Hendrik is third from the left.

Scott sits beside me. He whistles under his breath. "This is gonna be gaaayyy."

I can hardly hear him. All I see is Lesley, her sweet brown eyes, her braided hair. The music swells. When Lesley dives deep and then surges back up through the brilliant other-worldly blue to breach the surface, I'm sure that she *has* come from another world—Atlantis or Middle-earth—and has been sent just to me. My heart pounds. Is she looking at me? She is, isn't she?

David—I seem to hear her say—*I know that you suck at Little League and that You Strike Out EVERY FREAKING GODDAMNED TIME, like your coach yells, but I love you anyway. And even though Tommy Marzipretta, who always hits home runs, has been hanging around me lately, where is he to-night, David? He's not here for me, but you are.*

"Correction," whispers Scott. "This is *extremely* gay."

Lesley does a perfect tuck and roll in the water and comes up smiling. There's pressure behind my eyes and I scamper out of my chair.

"What's up?" says Scott, but I hurry away from the show. I cross the parking lot alone and run behind the greenskeeper's garage, onto the path.

A question the size of the Milky Way is in my heart. *Are you my wife, Lesley Hendrik? Are you?*

I get to my spot and stare into the woods, the shadows under the trees, below the fireflies.

Is she who I'm meant for? I ask the shadows. *Tell me, Lord. Tell me what I'll be.*

EACH NOVEMBER AFTERNOON, boys from Twin Circle Drive and Raven Road play football behind Washington Irving Middle School, which is nearby. Almost all the guys are Italian. There are the three Langini brothers, the two Barella brothers, Tommy and Tony Marzipretta, and Matt Argento, the oldest kid on Twin Circle Drive, who will play football in college someday, or so I am constantly told.

Most afternoons I'm on the path or home watching *Batman* reruns or wishing I had Atari. But I join the football games often enough not to be a tard. I am a generally tolerated member of the group when I show up. One Friday I stand in the huddle. Matt Argento is quarterback. It's Matt and I and the Barellas against the Langinis and Marziprettas.

"Minghia!" says Matt, smiling and rubbing his back. "They tackled me good on that last play." He claps his hands in the huddle. "Okay, let's go flea flicker. No, fuck that, let's go play action. Okay, break."

Since I never watch NFL games, I have no clue what he means. I just try to do what Scott does. At the snap the ball ends up in my hands and I run. I don't know how to juke or flick a flea but I get pretty far down the field considering the Marziprettas are both hanging off me. I have no moves, but I'm strong and fast like my father and I move forward as far as I can. *Schicklers aren't easy to knock down*, he has often told me.

"Minghia!" shouts Matt Argento now as we gather for another huddle. "That wasn't bad, Schickler!" He claps my back and I proudly memorize where his hand hit me. I will tell my father about this.

Tommy snorts. "Schickler's a Kraut pussy."

"He got thirty yards on your dago ass," says Matt.

He pats my back again and I feel even prouder.

The next morning, a Saturday, my father wakes me at four o'clock. I dress in a sleepy haze, get in the car beside him, put my face near the heat vent while he drives. We're driving to a diner in some woodsy nowhere place an hour from my home to meet my father's buddies for breakfast. Then we're all going turkey hunting.

On my grandfather's farm—which was just a mile from Twin Circle Drive before my grandparents gave it up—my father started hunting and trapping at three years old. He would crawl around in the woods at my age, smoking his pipe and trapping mink and fox. Then he'd sell their pelts to a traveling Polish fur trader named Mr. Daklis who had cracked brown teeth and who visited the farm once a month. Hunting-wise, my father still has down-home tricks, like he packs Cream of Wheat powder inside his shotgun shells among the pellets. He tells me that this tightens the spread pattern.

"And why do we need a tight spread pattern?" he asks now as we drive.

I panic, trying to recall previous advice of his. "Because . . . because turkeys' heads are so small? And because a head shot is really the only way to kill a turkey?"

He pats my thigh. "Exactly. You've got all the right instincts for this."

He is being kind. I have zero instincts for this. I carry a BB gun, but the only time I ever fired it at an animal was in our backyard. I pegged a sparrow in the wing and when it limped off into the bushes, I felt horrible and said a Rosary for it.

When we get to the diner, it is full of other hunters. Two are my father's buddies, and we sit and eat with them. They like jokes and coffee. They whisper about the waitress's ass. They don't think that I can hear them.

"I'd order that ass with hash browns on the side," one whispers.

"I'd order that ass with biscuits and gravy," the other whispers back.

My father likes these men—he grew up with them—but he wouldn't be caught dead whispering like they do. The waitress's ass isn't on his radar. He loves the Catholic Church and my mother and us kids first, and then General Motors, and then not too much else.

He is somehow always a man apart. When my mother and her siblings and their friends have parties at our house on winter weekend nights, my father will chat with everyone for a while, but then the socializing will get to be too much for him. Once, a couple hours into such a party, everyone started asking

"Where's Jack?" I went searching for him. In my parents' darkened bedroom the guests' thick winter coats were piled on the bed. I walked around this cozy mountain until I saw a peek of his arm sticking out from under the coats. I moved a parka aside and revealed his face. He winked at me.

"How come you're under there?"

"I'm resting. I'm thinking."

"Is it a secret?"

He said, "Yep, don't tell." And I snuck back out.

As a problem solver and authority figure, my father is equally unusual. When I was eight, he and I were out sledding one raw winter day on the steep tenth-hole hill of the golf course, and the hill was covered with neighborhood kids. I'd forgotten my face mask and I kept whining that I'd get frostbite. My father pulled out a tube of cherry ChapStick, held my chin, then Zambonied the ChapStick over my face, covering my cheeks and forehead with goop. Bam: problem solved, frostbite thwarted, and never mind that the other kids called me the Red Retard for the rest of the day.

Now, here at this diner, my dad's two buddies are whispering that powdered sugar and maple syrup might be just the things to sweeten up that waitress's ass. Finally my father clears his throat and his pals stop whispering. Problem solved, lewdness thwarted.

A strange man comes over to chat. He knows my dad's buddies. Also he drinks from a flask and reeks like fuel, which is ruining the smell of my fried eggs and ham.

In the car afterward, as we drive deeper into woodsy no-where, my father asks if I know what was in the man's flask.

"It smelled like fuel," I say.

"It was gin." My father winces. "Gin, before the sun's up? Ugh. David, when you get older, never drink gin. Schicklers don't do well with gin. Nobody does, really."

I nod. My father and I don't always talk much. What we usually do is, he will be in some room, trying to understand and enjoy life, and I will be in that same room near him, also trying to understand and enjoy life, and that is our connection.

Sometimes, though, I pepper him with questions.

"Dad?"

"Yes?"

"Why don't Schicklers do well with gin?"

My father sits up straighter in his seat. He does this when he's ready to teach me something. "Because the juniper berry is the worst kind of berry. The juice of the juniper, which gin comes from, is hard for the human liver to break down. It's like drinking pine resin."

"All right, Dad." I have no idea what the hell he's talking about—he is a whip-smart chemical and mechanical engineer by training—but I love his voice.

"Dad, what's play action?"

"It's when you set up for a run, but then you go to the air instead."

Go to the air. I will write this phrase down at home. I love words and books.

"And what's flea flicker?"

"What's *a* flea flicker. That's when you . . . well, that one would be easier for me to draw for you. Ask me again when we get home."

"Okay," I say.

A silence passes.

"Dad?"

"Yes?"

"How come in the woods at home Scott and I find broken china in the dirt?"

He straightens up again. "The land where the woods are now used to be a huge pig farm owned by the Muellers. Their family knew ours. Fancy restaurants downtown used to have clambakes for rich people, and afterward the restaurants would truck the remains out and dump everything. There were some bits of clams and the pigs ate those, but there were also chipped plates that the restaurant threw out. Now our woods have grown over all that and they're beautiful." He gives me a hard, proud look.

I come from a dump, I think.

"All right, Dad."

SOON IT'S WINTER. I sled each afternoon with Scott Barella and other Twin Circle Drive and Raven Road kids out on the tenth-hole hill. The sun sets by four o'clock and the only way to see is by the shine off the deep snow. The drifts are white in daylight but at this darker hour the glow off them is a subtle purple vapor that I love. After the other kids go home I trudge to my spot on the path.

Thank You, Lord, I pray. *Thank You for this odd and purple place.*

One frigid night when I'm standing there, I hear cracks like gunshots in the woods. Ice, somewhere close by, is shearing off pine tree branches. The sound makes me afraid of summer, afraid of the sun coming back. I worry each spring that the months of light ahead will kill the secrets of my dark path.

Instead, summer brings parties. My parents host burger cookouts in our backyard. In advance of these cookouts, my father and I tend our lawn religiously.

The lawn is our strongest bond, his and mine. When it comes to our grass, I do have instincts, and I feel like a farming man's son. I know how to vinegar certain weeds, when to fertilize. If the grass gets blighted or filled with mole runs, I lose sleep. If there is drought and the lawn burns out, part of me burns out, too.

Chewing on wild rhubarb stalks—but never on their poisonous leaves—I steer our John Deere riding tractor over our acre of land once every five days. If I'm not chewing rhubarb, I sing while I drive, usually Bruce Springsteen's "Rosalita," at the top of my lungs.

One sunny evening after I've mowed, my father is late for

dinner. My mother sees his car parked in the driveway. She and my sisters search around. Looking out our back window, they yell and freak out.

"There he is!" hollers Anne Marie.

"He's dead!" yells Pam. "Heart attack!"

I look out the window. Still in his suit and tie and clutching his briefcase, my father is lying splayed on the lawn, limbs everywhere, eyes closed. He looks like a man who took a bullet, but I know that he's just filling his nostrils with the smell of the deep, shorn green around him. He loves our land.

My mother loves people. She is the spark of the burger parties and all our parties. My father is German and his nine siblings are kooky farmer types who rarely see one another. My mother is Irish and she and her seven siblings—the Edds—party constantly. Her five brothers drink Genesee 12 Horse Ale. Their wives roll their eyes at the men and serve salads with strawberries trapped in Jell-O.

My mother is the center of it all. Every joke is funnier when she laughs at it and every baby placed in her arms stops crying. The Sermon on the Mount says *Blessed are the peacemakers* and that's what my mother is, a peacemaker. Actually I'm not sure that she makes it: I think it just comes naturally out of her pores and fills whatever room she's in. I watch her at one summer family party as she pours a glass full of beer and brings it to my great-aunt Clara, who comes up from Yonkers once each summer to frighten me and my sisters. Aunt Clara can barely walk. She is fat and addicted to Bingo and has warts and hairs on her cheeks. When my mother gives Aunt Clara the beer, Aunt Clara complains.

"It's too foamy, Peggy."

My mother blows off the foam.

"I hate Brooklyn, Peggy."

"I know." My mother rubs Aunt Clara's back.

Aunt Clara starts to weep. "I'm going to die."

"Nope." My mother kisses Aunt Clara on the cheek, right where she always does, on the nastiest, wartiest part.

Watching my mother do this, I think, *Be like that, David. Make peace and kiss warts. Be a priest.*

I run to find my young cousins. I am always in charge of them at these backyard summer parties. They are half a dozen little boys and girls, all under ten. On this evening I lead them into the woods. I show them the hole of the woodchuck that chases me when I pick rhubarb. I point out a hawk overhead.

"It would take a tight spread pattern to kill that hawk," I say.

"What's a spread pattern?" asks one cousin.

I don't know, so I change the subject. "I want to show you guys something."

I take them to the path. It's an August evening, close to twilight, and the woods smell like sweet alyssum and grape blossoms. The shadows among the trees are floating and shifting like a fragrant fog, and I wish that I could dive into their blackness and hang suspended in it.

I stand at my spot, point at the woods. "Pretty great."

"Stupid trees," says a cousin.

"Yeah, let's go back to the house," says another.

Sometimes I want someone else to see what I see. Other times I want to be the only one.

I'm TWELVE NOW and sure that my sisters will kill me. Or themselves, or all four of us. It will happen in the yellow bathroom, the kids' bathroom, in the upstairs of our house. My sisters don't have much in common: Anne Marie, the eldest, is our family's sole, freckly blonde who gets straight A's and bakes cakes and wants a boyfriend. Tall, dark-haired Pamela is all energy, bored at school except in art class. Jeanne is cute and small and has striking blue eyes that are often worried. The only things my sisters all agree on and will do side by side are dance or style their hair.

The hair styling is how they will kill me. Each morning before school or church the bathroom floor and sink counter are covered with water puddles because my sisters either forget to use the shower curtain or else their hair drips everywhere. Buzzing and hopping in the puddles on the counter are plugged-in, running hair dryers, curling irons, and hair straighteners. I try to mop up the puddles so I won't get electrocuted, but it's hard because time is short and I have to move fast to grab *my* chance to use the dryer and the mousse and the thick black Goody brush.

One Sunday before church, Jeanne stands in a puddle, hogging the dryer and singing Fleetwood Mac's "Gypsy."

"My turn," I say.

I try to grab the dryer, but she keeps it out of reach. We bang into Anne Marie, who bumps us away with her hip and goes on curling her hair. Pam is beside Anne Marie, putting on eyeliner.

"And stop singing," I tell Jeanne.

"Ha," Anne Marie says. "What about you on the tractor?"

"I'll sing when I want," Jeanne announces. " 'Gypsy' is my favorite song."

"You'll be sick of it in a week," I say. "You always get sick of your favorites."

Jeanne's face clouds. She is eight and sensitive. "I . . . I love 'Gypsy,' " she says stubbornly, her chin quaking.

"Enough, you guys," says Pam.

"Soon you'll hate it." I lean close so Jeanne will hear me over the dryer. "You. Will. Hate. 'Gypsy.' "

" 'Gypsy'!" Jeanne wails. "I love 'Gypsy'! FOREVER!"

She smacks the dryer down and I pick it up, satisfied. Jeanne is still crying. My parents poke their heads in and my father's eyes look ready to be angry. When he sees me teasing my hair back with the dryer and the Goody brush, he glances desperately at my mother.

"Everyone, downstairs," she says.

Minutes later, we're at breakfast. My sisters and I sit there with moussed hair and thank Jesus for our waffles. After eating we go to Mass. Technically Catholics shouldn't eat right before receiving the Eucharist, but my father always says that Schicklers get cranky when they're hungry.

I'm now the regular altar boy for Sunday-morning Mass. I sit on the altar in my robes and wash Father Anselm's fingertips and ring bells and light incense. Father Anselm still says *nifty* too often around me, and there are still people in bubbly-safe pastels and I still get headaches, but I'm being patient. I'm waiting for the God I pray to on the dark path to appear in church. If He and His darkness ever show up at Mass, it will be a sign that He wants me to be a priest, to worship Him from the solitude that I feel on the path. That's the deal I've made in my heart.

In the meantime, I spot Caitlin Brenner in her pew. When she catches my eye, I telepathically zap toward her the haiku I've been working on:

> *Caitlin! The best girl.*
> *I love how your blond hair shines.*
> *Go to a movie.*

I need to fix that last line. It should be "*Let's* go to a movie," but that would be six syllables instead of five, which is breaking haiku rules. Still, I watch Caitlin, in case what I just broadcast to her rocked her world. She looks away, giving her hair a haughty flip. That's okay, because I've secretly written another version of the haiku:

Lesley! The best girl.
I love how your brown hair shines.
Go to a movie.

Since it's October and Lesley Hendrik doesn't attend Saint Helen's, I haven't seen her lately, so I haven't yet telepathed the haiku at her and blown her mind. I will do so over Christmas or next summer at the pool.

After church my parents sit me down at home.

My mother rubs my arm. "David, Dad and I have been talking. And we have a surprise. We're going to build you a special bedroom in the basement."

"The basement?" I fret and think of fire exits. In my current second-floor bedroom there's a chain-link ladder in my closet. If a fire blocks us from the stairs, it's my job to attach the ladder to my window and get me and my sisters out.

"What about the fire ladder?" I ask.

"Anne Marie can handle that. Don't worry, your basement room will have a special, wide window with steps leading out."

My heart calms down a notch.

My mother rubs my arm more. "A boy needs his space. You don't need to always be around girl stuff. You're practically a young man."

Ohhh, I think. *I get it. Me and the hair dryer. Me and the mousse.*

I want to tell them not to worry, that I'm not homosexual, that I've started having *very* specific thoughts about Caitlin and Lesley's bodies. But I hold my tongue. They're offering me a Fortress of Solitude.

My uncle Travis, a carpenter, builds the room. When he's done, it's a wood-paneled den of a place. Before I move in I climb in and out of the fire window several times. Scott Barella clocks me and it never takes me more than five seconds from under the bedsheets till I'm standing outside in the freezing air.

I stay up late one night in bed. No moonlight makes it through my window. Even with my eyes open, I see total pitch-black in one corner. I snuggle under my blankets. The darkness feels hidden from the world, given just to me. I feel a great calm.

Is that You, Lord? I pray into the darkness. *Are You down here with me?*

IN JUNE WHEN I'm thirteen I graduate from eighth grade at Saint Helen's School and I win the Religion Award. I hadn't known there was such an award, and after I win it a guy in my class signs my yearbook, *Nice Going, Jesus Tard!*

When it comes to Jesus, I've always known what the Gospel says or what church adults want to hear. But I have a Jesus problem. According to Scripture, Jesus is the Light of the World. In the Gospel of John, Jesus says that He has come as a Light into the world so that we won't have to abide in darkness. Everyone makes it sound like Jesus is literally hanging out in the sunlight at Saint Helen's during morning Mass, like He's right there in the weave of the bright, nifty sweaters around me.

My problem is, I like abiding in darkness. I like the dark path, the low, forever shadows among the trees. For me, God is in that darkness. He's not a devil, or a tree, or a wood sprite. He's the Lord, He just happens to be in darkness. I feel restful knowing that He's there and I love Him, but I can't explain why I find Him where I do. I'm afraid to try. I'm afraid it's wrong. And I'm afraid that if I go talking about how God is in the darkness, He will leave it and I'll be alone.

One night that same June, Scott and I prowl through the country club woods, hunting for Tommy Marzipretta. We and some other kids are playing a chase-and-hunt game that we call Ghost-Ghost and Tommy is the ghost, the prey. I'm excited because Lesley Hendrik is playing and she's wearing her blue jeans with the tiny pink suede frog sewn on the butt pocket.

Scott and I have been searching for a while. We scuff along on the dark path. Rounding a bend, we come across Lesley and Tommy. They're near my favorite spot on the path. Lesley stands leaning back against a large maple tree and Tommy stands close to her. Also, they're not wearing pants and he's fucking her.

"Shit bomb," says Scott quietly.

27

I stop dead still. I've never even kissed a girl. I blink rapidly to make sure that those are Lesley's jeans lying disembodied in the grass. Yes, there's the pink suede frog. As for Lesley herself, her startling, pale white ass rubs up and down against the tree bark and I look at her startled, lovely face. Tommy casually raises his chin in greeting to us and keeps plunging into Lesley.

"Took you faggots long enough to find us," he says.

I can't breathe right. It's a sin to fuck a girl you're not married to, and it's probably an even bigger sin if you fuck a girl you're not married to up against a tree. And Tommy is fucking my Lesley on my path. There's a knife dicing me up inside.

More ghost-searchers wander up behind me. It's the Langini brothers and Lesley's best friend, Theresa Whelan, another Raven Road girl. They all see the rutting couple and stop.

"Minghia!" says Mike Langini.

"Yep," says Tommy. He stops thrusting and just stands there with his naked middle trapping Lesley's naked middle against the tree.

Theresa laughs her nervous laugh and waves. "Hey, Lesley."

"Hey, Theresa." Lesley waves back weakly. No one seems to know what to say. None of us except Tommy is even fifteen yet. Lesley looks like a specimen in science class, a butterfly spread and pinned to a board. I need her to feel embarrassed and terrified by what's happening to her, the way I feel, but she turns her face away so I'll never know.

"I'm inside her," clarifies Tommy.

I can't take it. I run home, alone. My mother and sisters are at a dance show, like they often are, and my father is in Detroit on GM business. When I get into the house I sit on the living room floor, anxious. I need release from what I just saw.

I go down to the basement, to the carpeted area outside my bedroom where we have a stereo and where my sisters work up their dance routines. I put on the *Grease* soundtrack and cue up "Summer Nights." Then I perform the routine that I—on previous occasions—have worked up to accompany this song. Dancing is what my sisters do to figure out their feelings and, when I'm alone, I sometimes do it, too.

I play the song through three times, performing the part that I've choreographed for Sandy, complete with falsetto high notes and skipping and flouncing. Then I play the song through three more times, performing Danny Zuko's part. Performing this girls-versus-guys duet is as close as I can come to processing thoughts about sex.

I am in mid-pirouette when the music cuts out.

"David?"

I yelp and turn around.

My father has his hand on the stereo volume knob. He's wearing a black suit and looking at me, astonished.

I pray, *Thank you, Lord, that I did Sandy's part first.*

"Dad . . . I thought you were in Detroit."

"I just got back."

I hug him and hold on for a while to let my blushing die down.

"David, what were you doing? Was that one of the girls' routines?"

I step back from him. "Sort of. I just . . . like that song."

He studies me. I know he worries that I act too much like a girl, but he won't freak out about my dancing. In our family we all love to cut the rug. At weddings my father jitterbugs with my mother, but he'll dance solo, too. During fast songs he has a move where he crouches down close to the floor and then shoots up, splaying out his arms and kicking, with a loopy grin on his face. When he does this, his stern authority melts and he looks joyful.

"David," he says now, "you look keyed up. What's the matter?"

In my mind I see the girl I adore getting fucked in the dark place I adore. There isn't supposed to be fucking on the path. Only contemplation. Only God.

"Nothing," I lie.

I GO TO an all-male high school, McQuaid Jesuit, and for four years I run cross-country. I do other things, too—tons of schoolwork, small chorus parts in a few plays—but cross-country is my obsession. The most addictive part of it is the Five Hundred Mile Challenge.

This challenge takes place in the summers. Our coach asks each of us to run five hundred miles over ten weeks to get ready for the fall season.

Each summer morning, rain or shine, I run three or four laps around the edges of Black Creek Country Club. Each lap is two and a half miles. I run shirtless, in shorts and Nikes. I run through woods, skirt the rough beside the fairways, climb grassy hills, and then run down into the cool pockets of air along Black Creek. I know every snarled tree root to dodge, every mossy or brittle patch of ground. I pound my feet extra hard as I cross the shoddy wooden bridge over the creek on the second hole, and the mother duck under the girders flaps out and bitches, *Seriously? Again? I've got kids here!*

At the end of each lap I zip through the woods and up the hill on the dark path. I can feel around me cool shadows touching my skin. I breathe these shadows in and they're more than oxygen, they're a dark essence thrilling my blood. When I charge along the path like this, alone, I feel words gathering at the tip of God's tongue. If I can just run fast enough or purely enough or with the whole of my being, He'll let loose the words. He'll speak and tell me my one sentence. He'll tell me my life.

Chapter Two

IT'S SEPTEMBER 1987, and my parents are dropping me off for my freshman year at Georgetown University. As they're preparing to leave, my father hugs me close.

"Don't get mono," he warns. "Schickler men are highly susceptible to mono."

"All right, Dad."

We're standing in my dorm room. My mother is getting something from the car while my father gives me last-minute advice.

"Have adventures." He pulls me close once more. I smell his aftershave and another smell that's just him. I've always loved the mix of these smells.

"I love you, David. Don't get mono."

"I won't."

A week later I have mono. I lie alone in my dorm room all day each day, missing classes, losing weight, spitting up blood, staring at my Morrissey poster.

I've never been so sick. My neck is hugely swollen, and any word I try to speak scrapes like a razor blade in my throat. Despite being bedridden, I can't sleep day or night. Even just raising my head off the mattress is a blinding-white mistake, so I just lie here, scared that I'm dying.

My father knew what he was warning me about. He had mono severely once and it almost killed him.

He too attended McQuaid High School, back in the fifties, and he worked his ass off there to get a full college ride to General Motors Institute. At GMI his nickname was Saint Jack because he got flawless grades and never slept around or did anything to impede his path toward marrying his sweetheart back home—my mother—and rising like a comet through the GM ranks. He pulled all-nighters in the library and lab, and this frayed him so badly one season that he collapsed with mono and ended up in the hospital.

I guess I've frayed myself, too. At McQuaid I did five hours of homework each night and graduated fourth in my class. Over this past summer I put in ten-hour days at an auto dealership to earn college tuition money. Weird older men customers kept gripping my shoulders and saying I was bound for great things. One imparted to me what he described as the key truth of living.

"A nigger will work for ya," he said, "but not a nigra. Learn the difference. There's niggers and nigras, and nigras are useless. Remember that."

Another man frowned when I told him excitedly that I'd spoken on the phone the night before with Adam Goldman from Bethesda, Maryland, my soon-to-be roommate.

"Adam Goldman," the man repeated. "I bet he'll be a very earthy and unspiritual person. They all are."

"Hoyas?" I asked.

"Jews," he said.

I LIE LIMP in my dorm bed, all energy sucked from my body. I've been here a month, but all I've seen of campus so far are my room's concrete walls. Painted pale yellow, they look jaundiced and sickly. They look like the mucus I keep spitting up.

"Do you need blankets?" asks my roommate. "Should I call the doctor again?"

Adam isn't earthy and unspiritual. He's kind and funny and on the football team. When his mom finds out about my mono, she moves Adam out of our room for a while, but she drives in from Bethesda with soups for me. My own parents, after dropping me in D.C., flew to Europe for a vacation, their first time abroad. They don't know yet that I'm this sick.

Each day the hundred other guys on my floor herd past my closed door, laughing and firming up friendships. I live in New South, a dorm of hard-charging strivers. One midnight as my throat aches there's a thump out in the hall, followed by love grunts. A toga party is raging downstairs in the common room and some probably-sheet-clad guy and girl are getting Roman up against my door.

"I'm going to fucking rupture you," growls the guy.

"Yes," begs the girl.

"Gonna split you in half."

The girl makes a sound of agreement. Then they're screwing against my door. Each time they bang against it I feel it in my swollen tonsils.

"Scootch me higher," yells the girl.

I send telepathy through the door. *Please don't scootch her higher.*

"Keep drilling me!"

Please stop drilling her.

"Oh yes! YEEEEEEEESSS!"

I put my pillow over my head. Who in the hell are these people? I try to imagine any girl I've ever met telling me, out loud, to keep drilling her. Or for that matter to *start* drilling her. I had a couple second-base experiences in high school, but I'm still a virgin . . . Saint David. I pull my pillow tighter to my head to drown out Orgasma Girl. Finally she and her battering ram move on and I sleep.

I dream of the path. I miss it: the Black Creek woods, the tart northern air, the shadows. Even from my dream, I pray to the Lord who somehow lives in that darkness back home. *Where are You in this new place? I'm sick. Please help.*

A voice cackles from above: "A-HAW-HAW-HAW-HAW!"

Is that You, Lord?

"A-HAW-HAW-HAW-HAW!"

I lurch awake. The cackling is music blaring from the room next door. My clock says two a.m., and the song pulsing through the wall is ZZ Top's "La Grange." It's the go-to song of the guys next door, Pike and Brett. They play it about thirty times in a row whenever they come home drunk, which is virtually every night.

I burrow my head under my pillow again. When the music quits, my room phone rings. I pick up but can barely speak a hello.

A male voice says sneeringly, "This is the SS."

The line goes dead. My ears, clogged with mono, are unsure of what they've heard until the phone rings again a minute later and I answer.

The same male voice says, "We are the SS. The train is coming for you."

I get similar calls for several nights. I'm enfeebled enough by the mono—and I guess innocent enough—not to comprehend what's up until one night when I force my pained vocal cords to answer.

"What's the SS?" I croak.

"Aw, fuck." The voice on the other end leans away. "Hey, man, I think it's the roommate."

"The Jew-mate," laughs a voice in the background.

"Whatever. Goldman's not there." The line clicks off and "La Grange" kicks into gear next door.

Pike and Brett, prank calling. Duh, Schickler.

When my mono's contagious stage is past, Adam returns to our room, but the late-night calls from the SS still come. After answering them, Adam often storms out and pounds on Pike and Brett's locked door, challenging them to come out and fight him. They never open up. They just guffaw at him from their cave. One morning after such a night, Adam helps me walk down to breakfast in the dorm cafeteria—I'm too weak to go alone—and there Pike and Brett are, showered, eating pancakes, looking like good little Boy Scouts. Adam could lay into them, but he sticks with me, his hand guiding my elbow.

ANOTHER WEEK PASSES and I'm still not well enough to leave the dorm—I get dizzy just stepping outside—but my voice has healed enough that I can talk on my room phone. One night I speak with my mother and sisters.

"You should've seen Dad at the airport when they got home," Pam says. "When we told him you had mono, he was so shocked and worried that he grabbed the wall so he wouldn't fall down."

"Don't tell him that!" calls my father in the background.

"He went white as a sheet," Pam continues.

There's commotion and then my father's voice takes over.

"David? How are you feeling?"

"I've lost twenty pounds and I look anorexic. But I think I've leveled off. I'll try classes Monday."

"Good." I can almost hear him nodding brisk approval. Then there's a pause. My father hates speaking on the phone, but I can tell that he has more to say, something to do with how pale he turned at the airport. "You're really out of the woods? Twenty pounds is a lot to lose. Do I need to come down there?"

"I'll be okay."

Another pause. He clears his throat, sounding normal again, relieved. "All right then. Go have adventures."

The next Monday I go to a political theory class. I'm in Georgetown's School of Foreign Service, which I applied to because my father said it would open up the world to me. This class is a two-hour lecture about Plato's Cave. I pass out cold twenty minutes in. When I come to, I'm shaking and nosebleeding onto my spiral-bound notebook. Some students escort me back to New South. I crawl into bed, exhausted and humiliated.

Days later I feel strong enough to hobble out again. This time I do so at night. I don't want to go far from New South in case I have another blackout, so I walk the hundred yards to Healy Lawn. It's two acres of grass in the middle of campus, with shrubs and trees and a fat pill of a moon overhead. It's the closest thing on campus to my woods back home.

I sit in the grass with the breeze on my face. Tired from just a stroll, my legs tremble in my jeans. Half a year ago I could run a mile in four minutes and forty seconds . . . now I have bed-sores on my ass.

The Healy tower gongs eleven o'clock. Minutes later I see a few students move through the Healy building toward Dahl-gren chapel. I follow them, curious why they're headed there so late.

Dahlgren is a red-brick building in a courtyard near a foun-tain. A sign outside the chapel advertises a nightly 11:15 Mass. I haven't been to church since arriving, so I go in. The chapel is simple inside, with dark corners, lit candles in the back, and chairs with plain red cushions. In the pews are fewer than a dozen students, all sitting up front near the altar. I sit near them but not among them.

The priest introduces himself as Father Michael Prince. He's tall and slight, with white hair and clear blue eyes. When he reads the Gospel he hunches over the lectern. His hands are frail claws that curl around the lectern's sides. His voice is a gasping whisper. Possibly because he looks and sounds as re-duced as I feel, I listen to him.

"Our faith isn't sorcery," he gasps. "Yet I'm asking you, in the middle of your classes and even in your coming here to-night . . . Is the magic there? Is there a glad danger calling you forward in life? There should be. God is that glad danger."

Afterward I hobble home to my room, thinking, *Glad dan-ger, glad danger.* The haiku writer in me considers writing the phrase down until . . .

"A-HAW-HAW-HAW-HAW!"

ZZ Top throbs in my sore tonsils, and the SS calls.

I go back to Dahlgren the next night, and the night after that. As I convalesce and resume classes, I show up every night. I've never been to Mass so late or met a priest like Father Prince. He's only fifty, but when he claws his hands around the lectern and preaches his spare sermons, he seems ancient, like a condor, like something that should be extinct but is stubbornly here.

He's a creature of night and his God seems to be, too. The shadows in the chapel corners, the handful of students in the pews, the way that Father Prince lights the incense and whispers the Agnus Dei, the prayer about Christ being the Lamb of God . . . it's all solemn and beautiful. There is nothing bubbly-safe about it. At these late Masses, when I receive Communion and I go back to my seat and kneel and shut my eyes, minutes feel like centuries. I feel God the way I feel Him on the path back home, only more so. I'm in a new quiet here, a new stillness. Each night when I pray I sense something—or feel or hear it, I can't quite say—in the darkness behind my closed eyes, maybe in my soul. It is something almost like a humming, something just this side of singing. If God is three persons in one—Father, Son, and Holy Spirit—maybe what I'm sensing is these three speaking low with one another, whispering. All of me leans forward, leans in, wanting to make out the whispers. To hear God's Voice.

My eyes snap open one night as I kneel in the pew. I stare at Father Prince and an ache in me says, *Really do it, David. Come here in solitude and listen for Him in the dark. Spend your life doing that. BE A PRIEST.*

The idea thrills through me stronger than it ever has.

Then I leap up, scared shitless, and get out of the chapel as fast as I can.

I HAVE FOUR new friends, the Alabama Boys.

They are two pairs of smart, funny roommates on my floor, all from the same state. In one room live Bob and Austin, and down the hall are Mason and Daniel. Daniel studies voice and can sing any girl out of her clothes, or so goes the rumor. New South girls also love Austin's peaches-and-cream accent and Mason's piercing blue Celtic eyes. It's only November but these three guys seem tight with half the chicks on campus.

As for the fourth Alabama Boy, Bob, he's dating Daisy McKay, who lives one floor below ours but sleeps in Bob's bed. Daisy and Bob have bat-shit crazy shouting matches over who just ate whose Cool Ranch Doritos.

On the night of my running-home-scared-from-Dahlgren-chapel, I reach Bob's room as Daisy is storming out.

"If you ever want sex again," she shrieks at him, "stop trashing Dire Straits!"

She disappears. I go into Bob's room to check on him, feeling glad for the distraction from my thoughts. The Priesthood Ache is still jangling through me and I don't know what to do with it.

Austin, Daniel, and Mason file into the room, too. I take up my quiet post in the corner. Bob opens his fridge, passes out Miller Genuine Draft longnecks, then turns on R.E.M.'s *Murmur*.

"Daisy's getting on my last nerve," he says. "I should fuck another chick to piss her off. Hannah Gorham, maybe."

"Hannah Gorham can't sing," says Daniel, who's starring in the fall musical.

Bob says, "Does a girl need to sing to sit on my fucking face?"

"Easy on the graphic talk," says Mason. "The gentle Schick is present."

"I'm not that gentle."

"Really?" Bob winks at the others. "I think it's time for Schick to play Who Would You Do."

Austin rubs my shoulders like I'm a prizefighter. "Let's hear it, Schick. Out of all the girls in the world, Who Would You Do?"

I drink my MGD, panicking.

Austin says, "Pick a girl on campus. A first-year, someone we all know."

"I ... um ..." My mind gallops. "Sitting Still," my favorite R.E.M. song, comes on. I like the Alabama Boys, but I'm nervous around them. They seem to belong to one another, and the beer and music belong to them, too. They seem in control of the ways they enjoy the world and I feel an opposite way. When I drink beer, like the MGD I'm holding, I belong to that beer while I'm drinking it. The same conquering thing happens to me when I hear "Sitting Still" or watch sunlight in the raindrops hanging from leaves on the Healy Lawn oak tree. The beauty of the world can own me.

"Our judges need an answer," says Bob.

"Um, Sara Draper," I say. "I'd do Sara Draper."

Bob snorts. "That flat-chested punk rocker from Darnell dorm?"

"With the dyed-pink bangs?" asks Daniel. "Why her?"

"Because..." I think it through. Sara Draper has elfin cheekbones. When I see her on campus, my heart asks, *Are you my wife, Sara?*

"I can't explain," I say.

"Damn straight you can't," says Bob. "Pick a girl with some curves and some tits."

Mason punches Bob's thigh. "Let Schick want who he wants."

A week later I'm out on Copley Lawn, next to Healy Lawn. I gape around at creation, grateful to be healthy. I do this a lot now that I'm out of my sickbed. There are crimson leaves on the trees, and frost on the statue of John Carroll, the university's founder.

"Hey," says a voice. "Hey, you're Dave, right?"

I look to one side and there stands Sara Draper with her nutty pink hair. She's smiling, drinking black coffee from a white cup. I almost touch her to make sure she's not a joke.

"You're Dave, right? I'm Sara. You sit near me in Map of the Modern World class. You had that awful mono, right? Are you feeling better?"

"Better," I manage to confirm.

"Listen, there's an M Street club I was hoping to go to Sunday night. Supposed to have great dancing. I thought we could go together. What do you think?"

I'm floored. I think, *I can't believe this is happening, Sara. You are pink and strange and I adore your cheekbones.*

"Church," I blurt. My voice is a squeak of panic. "I, um . . . I'm sorry, but I can't go to the club because I go to church on Sunday nights. The late Mass."

Sara gives me a look, knowing as well as I that there are about thirty Sunday daytime Masses I could opt for. "You mysterious Catholics." She smiles and walks off.

The Alabama Boys holler at me in my head. *Chase her! Tackle her! Drill her, and keep drilling her!*

I almost take a step in Sara's direction, then I don't.

THE PRIESTHOOD ACHE is a daily need, a fear, a confusion.

I want to be a good person. In my heart there's a path, a private way. It's a mysterious path, hard to discern, shifting with shadows, but it leads to the truth. It leads to less me and more God. It's the path of a man, not a boy. Growing up, watching my father, I learned that you have to be a man and know what your strength is. His strength, my father's, is green grass, morning Mass, our family, and General Motors. My strength is green grass, haikus, running, and pining for girls.

But my strongest strength, I think, is darkness. The solitary path. The Priesthood Ache. And the more that I know this, the more I want to look away from it, walk away, ignore it. Because I suspect that this path will have terrible demands. Costs.

IN FEBRUARY I get set up to attend the Sadie Hawkins dance with Mindy Falippis, the roommate of Daisy McKay. Mindy is in Georgetown's nursing school. She is fragile and emaciated, sort of like me, which is probably why Daisy and the Alabama Boys set us up. Under no circumstances, though, am I to make a major move on Mindy. Daisy tells me this in the New South stairwell before the dance.

"Mindy is special," Daisy warns me. "So behave yourself."

I stand itching under the collar of the tuxedo Mason loaned me. Unlike me, many of the guys on my floor own tuxedos, like junior James Bonds.

"Listen," Daisy continues, "Mindy wants you to sleep in her bed tonight, and you may. It'll be cute and nice for you both. But if you try more than a kiss, I'll hear about it and I'll castrate you where you stand. Are we clear?"

Daisy's lecture is unnecessary. Mindy and I not only don't kiss, we spend the night lying side by side on her bed, both fully clothed beneath the blanket. Mindy keeps her arms and legs ramrod straight, never touching me, while I stare at the ceiling until dawn.

A couple weeks later I have my only other "date" of the year. It happens late one weekend night when my roommate's away. I'm lying in bed when a large, drunken girl named Tabitha stumbles into my room, shuts the door, and lies on top of me. Her breath is bright with whiskey. I barely know her, but she shoves her tongue in my mouth.

"Missed you, Joey," she slurs.

"Tabitha, it's me, Dave. I'm not Joey, I'm Dave. This is Dave and Adam's room. You have the wrong room."

I try to squirm out from under her, but her body has gone relaxed and heavy on me, and my arms and legs are still fatigued from mono.

"Kiss me, Joey." Tabitha gives me more mouth-to-mouth. She's a girl and I'm lonely, so the kissing is nice. But I break my mouth away once more.

"I'm not Joey, I'm Dave."

"Blow you, Joey?"

Oh, my God. Her hand fumbles at my crotch. She unzips me, which no girl has ever done. Her head moves south.

Look, Lord! I think. *Trouble on Jupiter! Go check it out, Lord, we're all good here on Earth for a few minutes . . .*

A second later Tabitha is snoring on my stomach, out cold. I wait, hoping that she'll have some miracle revival. When she doesn't, I struggle out from under her. I find the freshman phone directory and call her roommate to come pick her up.

ONE NIGHT I'M in my dorm room talking with Mason, the Alabama Boy with whom I'm closest. We've shown each other poems that we've written. Tonight we're talking about books and authors.

"What about Kerouac?" I ask him.

Mason snorts. "Too in love with himself."

"Hunter S. Thompson?"

"Same."

We are both big on Ken Kesey's *One Flew Over the Cuckoo's Nest*. Mason loves the Southern giants, Faulkner and Robert Penn Warren. As for me, I'm in love with chapter three of *The Great Gatsby*, the one about Gatsby's mansion party on a shimmering summer night. I love that party so much that I need it to be real. I need to attend it, to hear the "yellow cocktail music" that plays at it. I tell Mason this.

He nods agreement. "We're both going to write like that, Schick."

"We are, huh."

"Yep. And it's going to get us laid."

Suddenly a hissing sound comes from the direction of my closed door to the dorm hall. A muffled voice on the other side of the door says, "Here you go, Jew."

A large liquid puddle spreads across my linoleum floor. The liquid is streaming in from under the door crack.

Mason points. "Is that piss?"

I leap up, but I'm barefoot and it takes me a second to step around the puddle and open the door. Whoever just pissed on my threshold has disappeared into the stairwell and is racing away, cackling.

Mason says, "Pike . . . that Nazi asshole."

Brett has calmed down recently, but not Pike. Lately he's been shaving off the eyebrows of guys who have passed out drunk in our lounge. It happened to my friend Rod and he wants revenge.

Meanwhile there's piss on my floor. Adam is in Bethesda visiting family, so Mason helps me clean up, and an hour later we're in my room again, talking, with the door closed. This time rather than hissing we hear retching, and then puke leaks in under the door crack.

Mason stares at it. "Are you fucking kidding me?"

I fling the door open and there's the shit-faced Pike, his fingers shoved down his throat, purging onto my doorstep. He grins and runs down the hall. I chase and tackle him. When I flip him over and kneel on his chest, he lolls his head and pukes more. It pools under his neck as I grab his shoulders and shake him.

"What the fuck is wrong with you?" I yell in his face.

His skull bounces in vomit as I shake him. His eyes are spidered with red glee and hatred.

"The Jew-mate," he whispers.

Our RA pulls me off Pike. Mason and I explain what happened and the RA orders Pike to clean up the vomit. Pike lurches his way back to my door. His mopping efforts last seconds, then he collapses giggling in the puke, rolling around in it. Mason and I grab his ankles, drag him next door, and heave him into his room.

AT MASS ONE NIGHT, Father Prince says that during our upcoming spring break, Campus Ministry will host a five-day silent retreat based on the spiritual exercises of Saint Ignatius Loyola, the Jesuits' founder.

"The retreat will take place," Father Prince says, "in Wernersville, Pennsylvania. It's remote and quiet. Many of you usually head to Fort Lauderdale, and I know what happens on that sort of vacation." He looks out at us in the pews. "But maybe some of you want a different kind of vacation. Maybe some of you feel called to . . ."

Is he looking at me? He is, isn't he?

". . . to something higher," says Father Prince.

I go to the Campus Ministry office. The retreat brochure says that the vow of silence involves no talking for five days, except for one short session per day with your priest advisor. It says that the silence might allow us to meet and hear God in new ways.

That hooks me. I want to hear God's Voice irrationally, totally, the way I want sex. The whispers I hear when I pray at nightly Mass make me impatient to move even closer to God, to hear more of Him. I twist my soul on some days to wring the Priesthood Ache out of it (*Priests never fuck!* I warn myself. *They rarely floss! Their breath stinks!*). But I can't shake it.

So I go on the retreat. I'm the only freshman who does. The retreat house is a country estate in the Pennsylvania hills. There are austere hallways and bedrooms inside, and outside is a footpath through forestland.

The priests running the retreat give talks. They tell us to imagine our way into Christ's life, to imagine that we're drinking wine at the Cana wedding feast, or seeing Lazarus walk out of his tomb. We're told to be specific in our imagining . . . How strong is the wine? What shade is Lazarus's skin? After such reflection, we're told to clear our thinking and go walking, to wait and see how God might make His presence known to us.

I do the reflections and walk on the footpath. It's late winter and early spring at once. The branches of trees are sleeved in ice, but the smell of growing things pushes up from the grass and shrubs. I breathe in the grounds. The footpath isn't as bewitching as my path back home, but it has good shadows. The silence—which I've observed for two days—is cool and clear around me and inside me. It reminds me of running, the silence does, because when I run I hone myself down to just flesh and breath, and this silence is a honing too, a switching off, an emptying out, an invitation to God to come fill that emptiness with Himself.

But I still haven't heard His Voice and it frustrates me.

On the third day we're each scheduled to meet with our assigned spiritual advisor for confession. I'm paired with Father John Wilhelm, a philosophy professor with crazy black hair. For the past two days I've said little in our sessions. In confession, though, I'll have to talk. I'm nervous. I haven't been to private confession in almost ten years.

In his talks to us Father Wilhelm has been serious but whimsical. So I write a list of my sins to bring to confession. I make it serious but whimsical.

The priest and I sit in chairs in a quiet denlike room.

"What's that you're holding?" he asks.

"A list of my sins. I'd like to read it if that's okay."

He nods. I begin to read. My list, arranged in two columns, is as follows:

MY SIN	ROUGHLY THE NUMBER OF TIMES I COMMITTED THIS SIN, 1980–88
Masturbated	1,000 times
Said "Fuck"	24,000 times
Said the name "Jesus Christ" in vain	18,000 times
Lusted after girls/women/ Lesley Hendrik	∞
Lied or white-lied	1,000 times
Was prideful	10,000 times

Fell asleep driving at night and
mangled a telephone pole with
　my dad's station wagon
　　(was sober, just tired)　　　　　　1 time

Gave an anti-Semitic jerk a
thrashing while he lolled
around in his own vomit
　　(am not really sorry)　　　　　　　1 time

I get maybe thirty seconds into reading aloud when an old feeling comes over me. A headachy, nauseous feeling. I stop speaking and stare at the notebook in my lap, the list. A point of pressure beads up in my forehead, above my right eye.

"Keep going," says the priest.

I can't. My list is bullshit. None of it is a lie, but it's bullshit anyway. It is nifty and pastel colored. It is bubbly-safe, a dilly.

Some part of me snaps its fingers in my face. *Quit fucking around*, it says. And then *pop*, one strong memory is in my head.

"David?" asks Father Wilhelm.

I sit there, caught in the memory. When I was a McQuaid junior, a senior named Jerry had an accident one spring day in the parking lot. He was riding on the hood of a buddy's car while the buddy steered around the lot. Jerry slid off the hood by accident, hit his head on the pavement, and died before nightfall. Though I'd been in the musical that spring with Jerry, he and I had never spoken. I went to his funeral with everyone from school.

After the funeral, a girl I knew from the Catholic girls' school near us—along with some of her girlfriends—picked me up and drove me to Lake Ontario for some distraction. And despite not having known Jerry and despite feeling no true sorrow at his death, I manufactured tears and hung my head during that drive to the lake. I felt fine, but to make the girls in that car cry and pat me with caring hands and whisper to me that I'd be all right, I put on a show of grief.

"David?" asks the priest. "Are you all right?"

"Father, I ..."

Maybe it was a tiny sin. But something like airplane turbulence is jolting my stomach. What I did wrong overwhelms me. A real human being, a boy like me, a son to two loving and devastated parents, died, and I capitalized on his death to boost my ego.

A sob lodges in my throat. I am so sorry that I can't meet the priest's eyes. Inside me, all the items on my list get swallowed up in God's darkness, *whoosh*, they're gone. I'm bawling, my chest heaving hard. It's partly relief, because I do suddenly feel forgiven. But I also feel like some cosmic vacuum cleaner just got turned on. I feel how entirely my dark God wants my love and wants to pull out of me the truth of who I am.

I drop my diary on the floor. Sobs rack through me.

Stop it, I tell myself. But I can't, and it's scary. As I cry, Father Wilhelm watches me in a way that I can't read at first. When I finish weeping, he hugs me.

"Schickler, there's not a competition going, but man, what a confession."

Afterward I walk alone on the footpath outside. My eyes are raw from crying.

Wait, I think. *What was that? That was real, but I couldn't steer it, and wait, wait, wait . . .*

DEEPLY SPOOKED, I hurry back to Georgetown almost as fast as I ran from the chapel that night last fall. I need a break from God, I decide. I need the Alabama Boys and springtime. And they're here for me. The weather warms, girls switch from jeans to skirts, and on Copley Lawn the cherry blossoms explode like sweet pink redemption. On my dorm hall another brand of redemption arrives one night when Pike is found passed out drunk in the lounge. Rod and Adam are summoned, and they go to work.

I don't know about it till the next morning when I'm coming back down the hall from the showers and I see a creature emerging from Pike and Brett's room.

"Whoa," I say.

The creature is wincing like he's hungover. His eyebrows have been shaved off, along with most of his hair. Tiny tufts of hair have been left on his skull like stubborn black crabgrass. Rod has also used black indelible marker to draw all over the bald parts. There are dark mushroom clouds and dark grim reapers and the giant words FUCK and CUNT and I HAD THIS COMING.

"Hi, Pike," I say.

He looks down and away as he passes.

A night later I go with the Alabama Boys to a house party off campus. Once we get there, the Boys melt off into the arms of girls. I find myself in a crowded kitchen. One guy is passing around giant plastic cups of Tanqueray gin and tonic to some girls.

"Want some gin?" he asks me.

"No thanks. The juniper berry is the worst kind of berry."

"What the fuck does that mean?"

I think about it. "I don't know. Give me some gin."

Soon I'm zippy on Tanqueray. I wander outside. On the back lawn stands a giant garbage can filled with rocket fuel, which is liquor mixed with cherry Kool-Aid packets. R.E.M.'s "Gardening at Night" plays on a stereo and I drink rocket fuel, feeling the springtime in my blood.

An hour later I'm somehow hanging out of a second-story bedroom window of the house, holding on to the window ledge with my feet. I'm not sure how I got here—a dare?—but I look down at the crowd on the grass. They're all walking on their heads. When I try to pull myself back up into the house, I can't. The crowd below drags the trash can of rocket fuel over underneath me.

"Go for it," someone calls.

"Into the drink!"

"Cliff dive, motherfucker!"

I try again to pull myself up into the window and can't.

"Help," I yell, scared now. "Someone help!"

Two guys I don't know scurry into the house and find the upstairs bedroom I'm in. Each grabs one of my feet. They strain, trying to reel me up and in. The crowd claps and shouts.

"Cliff-dive-cliff-dive!"

My right foot slips in its holder's grasp. "Don't let go," I beg.

Then I see Pike in the crowd below. He's not cheering, just looking up at me, his eyes locked on mine. With the mushroom clouds and the FUCK YOUs on his scalp and the leer on his face, he looks like the ringmaster of some apocalyptic circus. He's grotesque but riveting, almost marvelous, and I can't look away from him, and his eyes say, *You have this coming, too. A reckoning. Just wait.*

Chapter Three

BY SEPTEMBER of sophomore year I'm all but certain that I'll join the Jesuits. As priests go, they're a damned smart bunch. The ones that teach at Georgetown run an impressive gamut. There is the Mystic, Father Prince—my favorite—but there's also the Bodybuilder, Father Kelleher, who teaches acting and whom girls around campus call Father What-a-Waste because of his good looks and huge pecs. Then there's the Cut-Up, Father Raminski, who teaches economics and who gasps and falls on the floor, twitching like a heart attack victim, when students give especially stupid answers to his questions. These are urbane, funny men, very different from Father Anselm, the nifty priest I grew up with. Jesuits travel the world and some say "fuck" a lot and I often see Kelleher and Raminski sitting in the front-window table at Georgetown's finest restaurant, eating rack of lamb on the university's dime. I could get used to rack of lamb.

But I'm keeping my Priesthood Ache secret from everyone until I'm sure.

To hide my feelings of priestly vocation and to advertise myself as a Cool and Normal Guy, I start wearing a tie-dyed poncho everywhere I go. It's midnight blue with long sleeves and psychedelic ribs of color radiating out from the solar plexus. When I walk around campus, hippie types come up to pet my sleeves and give me mellow kudos.

One day, a week into school, I walk down O Street with an actor friend. I'm feeling tough and radiant not only because I'm in my poncho but because all summer long I painted houses back home in Rochester, so I'm tan and I have two rugged-looking scabs on my jaw where a coworker's electric sander grazed me.

The actor nods at a row house up ahead. "I need to stop in here and say hi to someone."

The sun is shining and making my jaw scabs tingle. "I'll wait outside," I say.

"She'll probably give us beer."

"I'll come in with you."

We go into the row house, which is tall, but so squished and narrow across that it looks lifted from a Roald Dahl story. The girl-who-will-probably-give-us-beer is sitting on her couch, looking through a box of mix tapes and laughing to herself about something. She's barefoot in jeans and a plain white

T-shirt, with waist-long straight and bright red hair. Her head is down, studying a tape cover. I can't see her face. Not having acknowledged us yet, she goes on laughing and the laugh is a low, brimming murmur that makes it sound like something is cooking and warming inside her.

The actor says, "Dave, this is Mara Kincannon."

"Hi," I say.

The girl looks up, smiling. She has pale, clear skin and her blasting green eyes knock my breath back down to my stomach. When her glance finds mine, her smile falters. The air between us gets goose bumps.

"Hey," she says softly.

The actor watches us staring at each other. "Uh-oh," he says.

THE HOUSE I grew up in was literally packed full of girls. Almost every weekend my two elder sisters had girlfriends sleep over, often for huge slumber parties. The guests were usually dancers, my sisters' fellow students from pointe, jazz, or tap. In our living room they'd push their pink and purple sleeping bags and all our furniture against walls and then choreograph and perform routines until three in the morning. In the years when I was five to seven or so, I was stuffed into leotards and thrown into these performances. I was given cameos while "Hey, Big Spender" or "Crocodile Rock" played on the stereo. If I made the girls happy, I would be group hugged. If I screwed up, I'd be banished to my bedroom, where I would grab my notebook and write disgruntled haikus:

You guys are unfair.
I am a good jazz dancer.
Let me back downstairs.

If Olympic gymnastics were on TV, our living room became a hushed church, with the girls and I in pajamas watching the screen breathlessly. The night in 1976 when Nadia Comaneci scored the Olympics' first perfect ten on the uneven bars in Montreal, my sisters and company wept for joy. Misty-eyed, I yelled to my father, "She nailed the landing, Daddy, oh, she nailed it!"

The Miss America pageant was a high holiday. The year I was ten, there must've been two dozen girls sleeping over on pageant night. They were twelve and thirteen years old now, and bitterly critical during the swimsuit competition:

"Gemma, check out Miss Oregon's suit. It looks like our costumes from 'Off the Wall.'"

"You're right. Sick. I hated my butt in that costume."

"We all hated your butt."

"Miss Florida has roots."

"Miss Delaware's voice is too nasal."

"Miss Nebraska has stork thighs. Gross."

I gazed at the TV screen, frowning. I thought Miss Nebraska's thighs were wonderful. Plus she'd played the flute well.

Plus, I hadn't hated Gemma's butt in her "Off the Wall" costume. I'd really appreciated her butt.

When these girls hugged me, their hair smelled like rain and strawberries. When they shrieked at one another, it meant they were angry or, more often, bored. They twirled around me year after year, and they did my face up like Ziggy Stardust with rouge and eye shadow.

Outside my house, close to me always, was the dark path and God. But inside my house, just as close, was the other great mystery: chicks. One autumn Saturday night when I was ten, I came home from a walk on the path. I'd been out talking to God about infinity. Infinity really screwed with my head and I was still going over some details of it in my mind with the Lord, getting a little pissed off at Him about it, as I came into my house and took off my boots and walked down into the basement.

Dear God, I thought, *if You really exist outside of time and space, that is messed up, because You haven't given us brains that can comprehend anything outside of time and space, and so haven't You made it hard for us to want infinity with You since we can't even imagine what infinity feels or looks like?*

I rounded a corner and found a dozen thirteen-year-old girls in nightgowns lying on top of one another on the carpeted floor, in two stacks, six to a stack, all of them laughing.

"We're seeing which stack will fall first," shouted someone.

"David, have you read *Mommie Dearest*?"

"David, push them over."

"No, push *them* over."

"David, sing 'Rainbow Connection.' I knooow it's your favorite."

"Hey, David," said my sister's friend Tina Cosgrove, who already had an amazing figure. "I hear you like Beth Vandermalley."

The other girls made teasing *Oooo* sounds at me.

I tried to defend myself. "Oh yeah, Tina, I hear you like Phil Kincaid."

Everyone shut up. Tina burst into tears. Her pile of girls fell and they all started patting her back.

"David, what the hell?"

"Yeah, David, that was mean."

Wait, I thought. *What? Not fair!*

Phil Kincaid was apparently a touchy subject. He'd spoken to Tina on Thursday but not on Friday. Disaster.

"Go away, David," said one girl, "you've done enough."

So I went into my room, my thoughts caught between infinity and nightgowns. *Dear Lord*, I prayed. *Tina Cosgrove is psychotic. And hot. Is she my wife?*

MARA IS a Georgetown sophomore like I am. She's from a small town near Kittery, Maine, and I happily suspect Catholicism in her family when she tells me that she has four sisters back home.

I start showing up at her row house each afternoon. One

day we sit on the couch and listen to an album by Joan Armatrading (whom Mara worships). Mara taps the scabs on my jaw.

"Where'd you get those?"

"Knife fight," I say.

She rolls her eyes.

"Lightsaber fight," I say.

"Come on . . ."

"One night last summer I broke into someone's mansion.
There was a guard dog Doberman and he lunged at my face.
He was out for blood."

She laughs her murmuring laugh and I want it never to
stop. Her laugh makes me gutsy. It short-circuits my shyness.

"And who lived in this mansion?" says Mara.

"A girl." I bump her knee with mine. "This amazing girl I
just had to get to."

She's sharing her row house with five girlfriends. It feels
like back home.

On an October Saturday, Mara and her housemates throw
a party. I arrive in my poncho. There are sixty revelers crowded
into a living room meant for twenty. The Housemartins blare
from the stereo, and Mara and some others teach me the drinking game Zoom Schwartz Profigliano. It's a weird blast of a
game, where keeping or breaking eye contact with people
makes you drink or not drink . . . but mostly drink. Mara
matches me shot for shot with the Jose Cuervo and by midnight, she and I are plastered and making out in the kitchen.

"Hold up a second," she says.

Leaning back against the counter, she removes her T-shirt and bra and stands topless before me. There are foodstuffs on the counter behind her, so what I see from left to right is: jar of flour, jar of sugar, Mara's naked breast, Mara's other naked breast, bottle of olive oil, box of Froot Loops.

Are you my wife? I think, looking at Mara. *Are you?*

She murmurs her laugh and we kiss again. Minutes later we've abandoned the party and we're in her upstairs bedroom. We climb onto the upper level of her bunk bed and fool around, holding things at third base. But a week later, on a night after a black-tie ball, she and I are naked in my Copley dorm room bed. I lie on top of her and keep my face buried in her neck as my body finds its way inside hers.

She grips me close. I crush my hips into hers and kiss her neck and come seconds later. We roll away from each other, both panting slightly.

"Okay," she says. "Okay." She has her back to me.

I wonder whether she was a virgin, too. The waterfall length of her hair fascinates me and I pet it. When it falls to one side, I see a scar at the back base of her neck. The scar has three small bands of raised skin like ridges on a washboard. I run my fingers over these ridges and try to make a joke.

"Help," I make my fingers say out loud. "I'm a ship caught in these river rapids. Somebody help."

Mara doesn't laugh.

"I'm sorry," I whisper, removing my hand. "What gave you that scar?"

"I don't know you well enough to tell you yet."

"Oh."

I go into my bathroom and sit trembling on the toilet. *Wait*, I think. *What? We can fuck, but I can't ask about scars? Not fair!*

I'm confused, flushed drunk with longing for her, and afraid. I decide that intercourse with her was a one-time thing, a mistake, a sin that will never happen again.

I don't see her for four days, but I think of her constantly. On the fourth night, I go drinking with Mason at an underground pub, The Tombs. We have good fake ID.

"You gonna visit her on the way home?" Mason asks.

"Hell, no."

"Dude, you know you want to see her."

I drain my mug of Rolling Rock. *David*, I think, *you're on a path toward solitude, toward God. You don't need distraction from that.*

Mason laughs. "You're totally going to her place."

"Fuck off, Mace."

We split a pitcher of Sam Adams and then it's two in the morning, and I'm weaving alone down the O Street sidewalk, or sidewalks, since there appear to be three of them. When I get to Mara's row house, her front door has been blown open by wind, which she told me happens sometimes. I chivalrously step inside and close the door behind me, because what if some drunk guy saw it open and just wandered in?

"Hello?" I call.

There's no answer, and this saddens me. I miss Mara. I have to tell her something vital, though I can't recall what. When I crawl into bed with her, I'll remember.

I fumble up the stairs and pause on the landing. There's one bedroom on the left, another on the right. I enter the latter, knowing that the top bunk in the far right corner holds Mara. I stand squinting in the dark at her bed, trying to make out her shape or the shape of her stuffed-animal toucan, Gabriel Puffalump. Her upper bunk looks higher than it did when we hooked up in it last week.

I cross the room and start climbing up to her. There are dresses and clothes hangers in my way as I climb, and I swat them aside. The hangers clatter.

A female voice gasps in the dark below. "Oh my God, who's there?"

I arrive on Mara's bunk. She's not there and neither is Gabriel Puffalump. Instead there are textbooks and women's hats. In a rush I throw these off the bunk, worried that Mara is trapped beneath them. The textbooks slap the floor below.

"What the fuck?" cries the same female voice. The voice isn't Mara's. "Who's there? What the fuck!"

"Where's Mara?" I finish clearing books off and lie down and close my eyes. The bunk feels hard, like a plain wooden slat, and it's thinner across than I remember, and there's no mattress, no blankets, no comfort.

"Mara," I wail.

"Wait . . . Dave?!" The female voice turns accusatory. "Dave Schickler?"

"Mara's not here," I moan.

"Of course she isn't! You're on the top shelf of my closet, you fucking idiot!"

The slat gives way under me. I fall through clothes hangers and hit the floor. Lights come on. I'm at the feet of Mara's housemate Melanie. She's standing in a long green nightshirt with her hands on her hips. There are textbooks and hats everywhere.

"You're in the wrong room. And you just scaled my closet. Are you on drugs?"

Mara comes in from the hall, from the direction of her bedroom, the one I thought I'd entered. She looks sleepy and beautiful. "Dave?"

My back is killing me. Mara lets me pass out in her bunk beside her.

The next day Melanie tells the whole campus about my closet climbing and I get mercilessly mocked. I vow to straighten up and fly right and be the kind of college student my father was. I try to put Mara from my mind, to crack down and study.

As a School of Foreign Service student, I'm learning German and taking required classes in diplomacy and economics. But these classes bore me. The only class jazzing me is sophomore honors English. We're reading *King Lear*, which I love.

It's elemental and urgent. When I read about Lear sprinting out alone into a dark wilderness to face the truth there, it feels like a sign.

So I start going to Father Prince's late Masses again. Each of his sermons is like a pail of cold water to my face. One night he talks about a time in his past during which he felt very self-satisfied.

"My classes and Masses were standing-room-only," he gasps. "Students hung on my words. They'd begun to see me as blessed and prophetic. And I'd begun to agree with them."

All of us in the pews laugh.

"Then one night I had a dream. I was teaching a class when the door blew open. Through the door I could see an immense darkness that all but poured into the room. I stopped teaching and stared into it, afraid."

None of us is laughing now.

"From out of the dark I heard a booming voice. Like a trumpet blast and a growl all at once. It said, '*Michael Prince . . . Michael Prince . . . The Bottom would like a word with you.*'"

The flesh on my arms prickles.

"That voice was God's, I'm certain of it," says the priest. "He was calling me out on my pride, urging me back to humility. But He was also revealing a frightening name for Himself. The Bottom. The Bottom."

This sermon hijacks my heart. I go about thinking of it nonstop. I know in my gut that the darkness that spoke to Father Prince was my darkness, the darkness of the path. And I know that the darkness, the Bottom, wants a word with me, too. God wants me to join a seminary, to pull a wild King Lear–like move and take Holy Orders.

I want to talk about this with Father Prince, but I'm scared to. I pace around on Copley Lawn one night, scuffing through fallen yellow leaves. Mason finds me.

"Hey, fuckface. What're you stressing out about tonight?"

I don't answer. I've never told him about the Priesthood Ache, but he's practically a mind reader.

"Schick, we've both got to go study abroad next year. Especially you."

"Why especially me?"

"So we can get you away from these goddamn Jesuits. Enough of this Catholic bullshit. You really believe that you're eating God's body during Communion?"

I say that I think so. I say that it might be a mystical body, but it's real.

"Then you know what that makes you, Schick? A mother-fucking *cannibal*!" Mason brays his wild laugh, but he's not kidding. "If this Catholic crap is so important, how come you're screwing Mara every other minute? Not that you shouldn't be."

I have no answer. I'm guilty as charged. Mara and I can't stay away from each other. We meet each night in the library. When we get hungry we quit studying and walk to a nearby deli to buy pasta and Paul Newman's red sauce and we go back to her row house and eat.

Afterward in her bunk bed we ravage each other. There's no moan that she makes that I don't carry down inside me. I'm falling for everything about her. After sex we lie naked, listening to music.

One night she puts on The Alarm's "Walk Forever by My Side."

"Really listen." She pets my face. "It's my favorite song."

I have my head resting on her abdomen, by her ribs. There's a scent to her skin here that I can't get enough of, a smell that's floral and lightly spicy. I want no man ever to have smelled it before me, just like I want Mara not to be agnostic, which she has said that she is.

"Why's it your favorite song?"

"It got me through a hard time."

"What hard time?"

She just goes on stroking my jawline.

"Where are you spending Thanksgiving?" I ask.

"Shhh. Just listen."

I can't see her face. There's nothing in the darkness but her body and mine and the warm white sheets. Her hair crackles with static electricity when I touch it. I graze my fingers over the back of her neck now, feeling her river-rapids scar. She still hasn't said how she got it.

"I love you," I say suddenly.

Her fingertips stop on my face.

"I love you, Mara. Please don't be mad that I'm saying it. I can't help it. I'm in love with you."

I get my head beside hers on the pillow and look at her. She gazes back with panic in her eyes and each second that she doesn't say it back to me is torture.

"David, please. I'm not ready for . . . just listen to the song."

PARENTS' WEEKEND ARRIVES in November. My parents drive down from Rochester. I stand at the campus gates on a Friday, waiting. When their maroon Buick pulls onto 37th Street, I see my mother's face through the windshield and she sees me and I imagine that she just knows.

"Jack!" I hear her cry. "Look at him! Oh God, I can see it . . . He's fucked somebody! Noooooo!!"

Of course she's really just smiling at me and waving as my father parks along the curb. I wave back.

As far as my parents know, Mara is just someone I've taken out a few times. Telling my mother what I've done with Mara would make my face explode. But looking through the windshield at my father, I want to tell him the truth. I've never kept crucial things from him. I've always felt like it would be unmanly, and maybe I feel that way because he's the strongest, most manly person I know. And the strongest thing about him is his love for my mom.

It is storybook strong, their love. Growing up, I saw it each night when my father got home from work. After removing his coat he would pull my mother to him. Closing his eyes he'd hold her tight and groan, sometimes for minutes, and I could hear in those groans his letting go of the world, of everything outside him and her. He occasionally threw in hammy growls to make us kids laugh if we were watching, but I knew that those groans came from his soul, and that those embraces recharged him.

That's marriage, I thought, watching. *If I ever have a wife, that's what I'll have.*

Now as I stand at the gates and watch my parents walk toward me, I'm wondering, *Will I groan like that for you, Mara? Will you Walk Forever by My Side?*

I take my parents to my dorm room. While my mother gets on the phone to make us dinner reservations, I play for my father the Joan Armatrading song "The Weakness in Me." It's on a mix Mara made me and I'm trying to drop hints to my father about the new path my romantic life has taken, a path full of, if not weakness, then helplessness on my part.

"It's a powerful ballad, huh, Dad? She's having a hard time choosing whether to take a certain lover."

My father looks confused. "Who is having a hard time?"

"The speaker of the song," I say.

"Why do you call the speaker 'she'?"

"I guess because Joan Armatrading is a woman."

He frowns. "Who is Joan Armatrading?"

"The woman singing the song."

"I think you mean *John* Armatrading."

"Um, her name is Joan," I say. "This is on a mix tape, so I can't show you her picture on the album, but—"

"That is a man singing," my father says.

"She has a deep voice," I say, "but she's definitely—"

"David." My father uses his end-of-discussion tone. "That.
Is a man. Singing."

Hints are not working.

So I decide to tell my father the flat-out truth about Mara
and me. I wait till I'm home in Rochester for Thanksgiving.
One night when he and I are in the house alone, I go into the
living room where he's watching television. I turn off the TV
and face him. My palms are shaking.

He's lying on the couch, but when he sees my expression, he
sits up. "David, what's wrong?"

"Dad." I swallow. "Dad . . ." I stop talking. It seems like
enough that I've affirmed who he is in relation to me.

"David, for God's sake, *what*?"

"I've been sleeping with Mara. Having sex with her."

He looks surprised and mad and worried for me all at once,
the way he did the night I barreled his Pontiac into a telephone
pole. "David, we're Catholic! Catholics stay chaste until they're
married!"

"I . . . I know that, I just—"

"Oh, son, we've got to get you to a priest."

I want to talk to you, I think.

"You need absolution."

I look at his feet, three sizes bigger than mine. He wants to
send me off to a rote sacrament, but I want to explain about
Mara, and her laugh, and the smell of the skin over her ribs.

"All right, Dad," I agree.

I go to confession that weekend and receive absolution from Father Harris, a priest our family knows. He's short and quiet and known for having a gift of healing, and I ask him why people shouldn't have intercourse before marriage. Father Harris blinks his peaceful eyes. He's pissing me off because he lives on some island of calm thousands of miles away from me and the rest of us.

"Because it is not God's will for us," he says.

I nod vaguely, thinking of Mara's slender thighs, planning the kisses that I'll give those thighs soon.

"All right, Father," I say.

I get back to Georgetown two nights later. There's a welcome-back card from Mara taped to the outside of my dorm room door. I rip the envelope off and open the card to read a sentence written in Mara's cursive, a sentence that I hoped for during all the dance recitals and water ballet concerts I ever attended.

I love you, David.

I shout out loud and sprint to Mara's row house two blocks away. When I come clattering through the door, she's standing there, waiting for me.

"You wrote *I love you*." I'm still panting.

She blushes. "It took me forever to write that down."

"You love me?"

She nods. I start toward her, but she holds up a hand to stop me. "It was cancer."

"What was cancer?"

"I had leukemia at the end of high school. I didn't know it for a while, but then I started passing out everywhere. One time I blacked out at school and fell down some stairs and cut the back of my neck open, and that's how I got my scar. When I went to the hospital for stitches, they ran tests and found the cancer." She is blurting all this out quietly, quickly. "And I couldn't tell you where I was going for Thanksgiving because I went to the town I grew up in back in New Hampshire to be in a protest and I didn't know how you'd feel about that. Our house back then was by a toxic waste site—none of our parents knew what it was—and lots of neighborhood kids got sick. Then it happened to me. So I went with my mom and sisters over Thanksgiving, because we think that's where my leukemia came from and we want that place shut down. We did a picket protest and got on the news. And I'm sorry it took me so long to say I love you, and I'm sorry if my rapids scar is gross for you to have to see. I'm sorry if touching it is . . . is gross."

I'm frozen in place with panic. "It's gone?" I'm pleading more than asking. "The cancer, it's—"

"It's in remission," she says.

I should've been there. I should've been there in the hospital with her, and at the protest. It cuts me like shattered glass in my stomach that I wasn't there.

"If you ever say that you're gross again . . ." I'm unable to finish the threat.

"I love you," she says.

I say that I love her. Then she kisses me and we go up to her room.

IN THE COMING DAYS I skip more classes than I attend, unable to crawl out of bed with Mara. How can my father or anyone ever know what she and I feel for each other? Has my father or Father Prince or God Himself ever had leukemia and beaten it and then made love with someone to show the universe that they've chosen the opposite of death? No, but Mara has, and we're sharing in the glory of each other.

Over Christmas I drive to Maine to visit Mara and her mother and her four sisters. Her parents are divorced and her dad still lives in New Hampshire, so I don't meet him. Mara's is a family of women, like mine, and three of Mara's sisters are older than she, each a New England beauty. One has two small daughters who call me Aunt Dave since they're used to having only women around. Another sister of Mara's looks so much like Mara that I have fantasies of sleeping with her, too.

Though it's December, Mara takes me walking on a beach just north of Kittery. In summer it caters to locals more than tourists and Mara is proud of it. She used to wait tables at the famous Witchmoor Inn nearby and she brings me there to meet the family who runs it. We drive up and down the coast and eat in dives, ordering steamed clams and beer in chilled mugs. We take beach walks through winter fogs that are touched by sun but that never burn off. We zip ourselves into a sleeping bag on her sister's living room floor one night and we have sex clandestinely, while her sister sleeps in the next room.

BUT INSIDE I'M confused, not at peace. When I'm alone in church now, my mind and heart wander toward Mara. Yet when I'm with her, I miss God and the dark, weightless time I spend alone with Him at Mass. Mara and I will be making love in her bed when the thought will land in me, *whump*, that what I'm up to with this girl has God mixed up in it whether I want that or not. Mara is on the pill, but fucking her still has a forever promise built into it, a promise that scares me.

I talk about all this with no one. Instead I try to love God and Mara in fierce parallel, to keep them distinct from each other by doing extremely religious things for God and extremely romantic ones for Mara. I get obsessive on both fronts.

Some Catholic friends tell me of the Croatian town of Medjugorje, a mountain village where, beginning in the early 1980s, the Virgin Mary allegedly started appearing to six young people and telling them how humanity could return to God. I don't know if I buy the story, but the visionaries say that Mary is urging mankind toward fasting and this intrigues me. Like darkness and silence, fasting sounds like a honing, an existential stripping away, an emptying out of myself . . . so maybe it is part of the path.

I try it. For twenty-four hours each Wednesday and Friday I ingest only water and bread crusts.

But the fasting only makes me starved for pleasure. Each Wednesday and Friday night I sit on Mara's couch, watching the clock till midnight. Then I wolf down Lipton butter noodles, haul Mara into her bedroom, and have at her.

Soon any small thing Mara likes becomes a mission for me to acquire. She likes a Steiff stuffed-animal bird in a shop window: I sneak back alone later that day to buy it. She mentions an obscure Genesis song called "Your Own Special Way": I scour grimy record stores, buy the album, and make Mara a mix tape.

On her birthday morning in April, I cook her homemade blueberry muffins, using my mother's recipe, and I appear in Mara's bedroom with a tray bearing the Steiff bird and the muffins.

"Surprise!"

Mara opens her eyes sleepily. "What? Hi, honey . . ."

"Happy birthday! Listen to *this*!" I pop the tape into the stereo and press play. A song begins. "It's 'Your Own Special Way'! And we're going on a picnic!"

She yawns. "Can't we just stay in bed?"

"No!"

I've borrowed Adam Goldman's car, and I drive us to Rock Creek Park in D.C. In the trunk is a picnic basket that I filled with sandwiches and a bottle of wine shaped like a fish that I bought because Mara once pointed to a bottle of wine shaped like a fish in a store window and said: "Kinda cool."

On the picnic we enjoy ourselves. But even the perfect setting and the hip wine bottle can't make things between me and Mara as perfect as I have been willing, or cosmically demanding, them to be.

A few weeks later, one night when we're in bed, I can't hold inside anymore what's been bothering me.

"Mara."

She hears the fear in my voice. "Honey, what is it?"

"I'm too ashamed to say it."

She locks her arms around me. "There's nothing you can't tell me."

"I have to stop. I can't go all the way with you in bed anymore."

She strokes my cheeks. Her expression is puzzled but accepting. "Okay."

"I—I hate that this is the case, but somehow—somehow me giving all of myself to you in full-on sex is something I can't handle, not till we're married. I'm sorry."

I say that I know that she might blame the Church and I tell her that I want to be like our friends, who seem to have no struggles with sex, but I say that I do have struggles with it, that it touches on God and my relationship with Him in overwhelming ways, and I say that if she's angry, I'll understand.

She hugs me. "I'm not angry, you dolt."

I promise her that we can still get wild and crazy and climaxingly naked together. I promise her that I love her.

"I love you too," she says.

Then we put on The Alarm, since that's something we can both believe in.

Chapter Four

MARA AND I sit on the ground in London's Trafalgar Square, holding hands. It's a bright day in late September 1989. The sun warms the gray bricks beneath us. Tomorrow I'll head to Tübingen in West Germany for my junior year abroad, a year which Mara will spend in Florence, Italy. We're having a last weekend together in England before launching our separate expatriate adventures.

"Check out that girl." Mara points to a couple our age standing beneath Lord Nelson's Column. The guy wears jeans and a black muscle shirt, while the girl has kinky red lace-up Doc Martens, a tight white bustier top, and black hair razored short. She's leaning up to her guy, whispering in his ear.

"She's doing what I do to you," Mara says. "She's using her feminine wiles to get what she wants."

"Why are wiles always feminine?" I ask. "That makes it sound like women are scheming behind the scenes, like courtesans. Can't I have masculine wiles?"

She squeezes my hand. "Yes. I'll always respect your masculine wiles. In fact I'll shorten the phrase and that's your new nickname. Max Wiles."

I kiss her knuckles.

"I'm going to bear your children," she says. "I'm scheming behind the scenes."

"I am, too."

"I'm afraid of this year," she says. "I'll miss you with everything in me."

I tell her that sometimes I miss her that way even when we're together.

Thirty-six hours later I'm alone on a train heading south from Frankfurt. It's late at night and there are no other passengers. My destination, Tübingen, is a university town in Germany's Baden-Württemberg region, in the country's southwest. I've never been there, but I've decided that the town will be quaint, and that my year here will be a perfect fairy tale, a break from real life.

I stare out the window. The train chugs past a moonlit field in which a cow stands by the tracks. The cow looks at me. Without opening its mouth it says, *Be a priest.*

I close my eyes. *Shut up, cow. You're part of Germany, so your job while I'm here is to be quaint, not prophetic, okay?*

When I open my eyes the train is passing a towering section

of the Black Forest. I look out at the forest. *Be a priest*, say the trees.

Shut up, Black Forest. What part of this-year-is-my-break-from-real-life didn't you understand?

But the Black Forest is bigger than a cow and the train isn't hurtling past very quickly, so the Forest answers, *You know you'll be a priest. When you're alone, you know it. Stop fooling around with Mara. You can't run from God, David.*

Watch me.

The conductor enters the car and takes the ticket I bought in Frankfurt. About seventy, he has a sturdy build and a snazzy conductor's cap. I smile, ready to let him inaugurate me into my fairy-tale year. Unfortunately he speaks Schwäbisch, a dialect I don't know, and I can babble back to him only in Hochdeutsch. Only later in the year, after listening to others speak his dialect, will I be able to cast back and parse out his increasingly frustrated words. Here they are in English:

TRAIN CONDUCTOR: (*studying my ticket*) This is out of order. This is totally wrong.

ME: Heartfelt greetings . . . I will study at the Eberhard Karls University of Tübingen.

TRAIN CONDUCTOR: (*waving my ticket*) You bought the wrong kind of ticket.

ME: I am very pleased and excited . . . I am the first from my family to study here.

TRAIN CONDUCTOR: This is totally wrong. You bought the

wrong kind of ticket. (*He points out the window.*) You must get off this train at the next stop.

ME: (*looking where he's pointing*) I too like to look out the window and witness the beautiful countryside.

TRAIN CONDUCTOR: You must get off this train at the next stop.

ME: What was that about the next stop?

TRAIN CONDUCTOR: (*taking me by the shoulders and steering me unequivocally toward the door*) At the next stop, you will leave.

ME: Whoa! Wait . . . is something out of order? Is something totally wrong?

At the next stop my bags and I disembark. At the station house I buy a ticket that to me looks identical to the out-of-order, totally wrong one, then I wait on the cold platform for a few hours, get on the next train and it takes me to Tübingen.

IT IS THE YEAR of Graham. He's a fellow Georgetown junior in the German study-abroad program, and we both get assigned to live north of the town of Tübingen in a student dorm called Waldhäuser Ost.

Graham is a ruddy, hot-tempered guy with blond hair and a fast, hard laugh. He's strong and built like a bear. He loves to cook and eat enormous meals. He sleeps late in an always dark-ened room with a mask over his eyes and he growls each morn-ing when I wake him for us to catch the bus down to the university.

We take classes together and we're stunned at how badly we suck at understanding our professors' German. During our en-trance exam Graham and I and other Americans are made to listen while a proctor reads a story called "Der Delphin" (dare DELL-fain), which we must then summarize in written Ger-man. I write a three-page essay about the oracle at Delphi, but it turns out that *der Delphin* is a plucky little dolphin trying to avoid commercial fishing nets. I barely get matriculated.

Graham hoots when we get our tests back and he sees the red-ink question marks all over my essay. "Nice work, Schick."

"Fuck off," I tell him.

We both love the blues music of Lightnin' Hopkins and we listen to his CDs while we play cards. We get plastered on pil-sner most nights and go out to see dubbed-German movies like *Harry und Sally* or *Sex, Lügen und Video*. When we get back to the dorm I squirrel myself away and write Mara haikus like this one:

Pale cool Irish girl
with green-fired eyes and tart tongue.
Italy loves you.

Or this one:

> *The world's shouting but*
> *our bodies pulse like Quiet.*
> *Stay inside with me.*

I send these poems to Mara in love letters. I miss her terribly, but after mailing the letters, I usually come back to my dorm and linger in the hall outside the communal kitchen, hoping to see Audrey and Nicole, the two girls who live on my floor. I'm still always in thrall to women living close to me.

Audrey is French and Nicole is Tunisian, and they're exchange students, too. Both are smart blondes who speak fluent German. Audrey has sad brown eyes and a just-out-of-bed languor to her movements. In the kitchen she and Nicole smoke together for hours. They laugh at my jokes and correct my German language mistakes. I admire the muted kitchen light in Audrey's hair, and she winks at me through the smoke rising from her Gauloises cigarette, and my heart asks, *Are you my wife, Audrey Vaillant?*

Each day after classes I wander in Tübingen's Altstadt, the Old City. There are fairy-tale details—cobblestone streets, buskers playing accordions—but I move past them alone, nervous about talking to natives and somehow just plain nervous anyway. I have a new unsettled dread in my blood. It's not loneliness for Mara or God because when I yearn for them, there's usually goodness—some sweet ache—to the yearning. This is

Something Else, this other feeling. There's nothing good about it. It isn't vertigo exactly, but it makes me feel like solid ground isn't there beneath me.

To shake the feeling off, I hang out with Graham. Every morning we go to the *Bäckerei* near our dorm and eat warm *Kirschtaschen* with ice-cold milk. Graham has been growing out his thick blond hair, with a beard to boot. He grins at me one morning as we chomp our cherry pastry.

"You know who'd enjoy this?" he says. "*Der Delphin.* Yes, if the dolphin prophet oracle were here, he'd devour these *Kirschtaschen* and tell us of our fates."

I punch him.

Days later I'm out running on a forest path near the dorm when I turn my left ankle hard and fall. Unable to run now, I hobble to the dorm and collapse in a chair in the common room, where Graham is riveted to the television. It is November 10, 1989, and the TV is tuned to the falling of the Berlin Wall, which began yesterday.

"We've gotta get up there," says Graham reverently, watching the images of people dancing atop the wall. "We'll hitchhike. We'll leave first thing in the morning."

"I can't. I just fucked up my foot. Twisted my ankle."

Graham shoots me a look. He and I have become so inseparable that Audrey and Nicole now just call us Dam-and-Grave.

"Just rest it tonight. But we're going, period. This is historic shit, man."

So I agree and go to call Mara (we speak rarely, since calls are expensive). The floor phone is a communal one in the hall. When I talk on it, I hunch over for privacy.

"I miss your river rapids," I tell Mara.

"I miss having you navigate those rapids," she says. "Listen, I've decided our first daughter will be named Mavis, after my sister, and maybe our first son will be Connor. Connor is negotiable, but Mavis is too cool a name to pass up."

It is cool, but I don't say so.

"Something's wrong, Max Wiles. Out with it."

"It's nothing . . . I've just been . . ." *I'm going to be a Jesuit*, I think. *There will be no Connor and no Mavis.* "I hurt my foot running, that's all. It's swollen."

"Then go ice it. And take some ibuprofen. Girlfriend's orders."

We hang up. In the dorm kitchen, I fill a bucket with ice and cold water and put my ankle in. Audrey wanders in and sees me.

"Oh, Dave . . . *was hast du getan?*" *Dave, what'd you do?*

I tell her about Berlin. She counsels me against the road trip. She's wearing silky, revealing blue pajamas and smoking, and I can tell from her breath that she just brushed her teeth. I try to keep my thoughts loyal to Mara, but Audrey keeps chatting with me and being lovely and French, so soon I'm fucking her senseless on a Saint-Tropez beach in my mind. After her twelfth orgasm, we swim in the waves. Then we plan our Notre Dame cathedral wedding, during which the music will be *Flying Cowboys* by Rickie Lee Jones.

"Dave? *Hast du mir gehört? Ich glaube dass du deine Reise nach Berlin absagen sollst. Dein Füss ist sehr verletzt.*" Dave, did you hear me? You should cancel your Berlin trip. Your foot is too hurt.

I blink, come back to the moment. I've never even kissed another girl behind Mara's back. Audrey smells like smoke and mint toothpaste and she tilts her head, letting her hair fall to one side in blond disarray. I'll never sleep with her, but she'll still go home to France next summer with a sliver of my soul tucked in her silk pajama shirt pocket.

On Saturday of that same weekend, Graham and I arrive at Berlin's Brandenburg Gate at midnight. The crowd is a singing, drinking mob. Graham brought a pickax and this makes us minor celebrities. Each person we meet borrows our weapon and hacks off a piece of history.

We haven't been in the crowd even an hour when my ankle starts killing me. It flares up so hugely that my swollen foot strains out of my sneaker. I try to drink enough Warsteiner beer to drown the pain, but standing up is almost unbearable. I sit on a curb to rest and watch the happy tumult. CNN, a fairly new TV network, is filming nearby. An East German man emerges from the crowd, beaming at me, carrying a dozen oranges in his shirt hem.

"You are American?!" he demands happily, in English.

"Yes."

"Look at me! Fruit! Huge moments!"

I laugh. There have been reports that those crossing over

are being given token gifts from West Berliners: some citrus or a few West German marks.

"Gratulieren," I tell the man. *Congratulations.*

He hauls me up to my feet. *"Tanzen wir!"* *Let's dance!*

"I can't..."

He spins me around a couple times, gripping my arm with one hand and holding his oranges with the other. I try to keep smiling, but the pain in my foot is excruciating, and he eventually sees my swollen sneaker.

"Oh," he says. "You are broken."

He pats my head and wanders off.

I'm a buzzkill, but it's no use. I hobble a long mile through the masses back toward my hostel bed.

Graham lets me lean on him as I limp along. "Don't give up, Schick. Would *der Delphin* give up?"

I grin at him, but the stabbing sensations in my foot get sharper and sharper. And beneath the pain but in league with it is that unsettled dread, that groundlessness I've been feeling. As I hobble along, this dread seems to whisper, *You* are *broken, David. And I am coming for you more fully. I am still a long way off, but make no mistake. I'm coming.*

MY ANKLE HEALS and my father visits Tübingen. He has just come from conducting some General Motors business in Frankfurt. We meet by the Tübingen town hall, hug hello, then go to a nearby tavern and get a table. I tell him about my classes until the waitress comes.

My father nudges me. "David, I think we're about ready for our first beer together."

His voice has a Rite of Passage tone to it. Sometimes when I was young he'd give me a sip of the one Grand-Dad Old Fashioned cocktail he would have each night when he got home from work. He never had two or more, and he told me once that he'd never been drunk in his life, that he'd never needed to be. I absolutely believed him. Meanwhile, he does not know that I have hung from windows drunk on rocket fuel or that I got plastered and horny and climbed a closet to search for my Mara.

"All right, Dad," I tell him.

I order for us. The waitress brings two Weizenbocks. We clink glasses and drink.

He says, "I've been wanting to share something with you, son."

My senses prick up. My father usually addresses me as "son" only if there's trouble.

"I've decided to become a deacon," he says.

If there were beer in my mouth I'd do a spit-take. "What?"

"I've already taken my first class and over the next few years I'll take the rest, getting my master's in theology and preparing for ordination."

In Catholicism, deacons are men (and only men) who serve

in a role beneath priests. Deacons—who can be married—can preach the Gospel, deliver homilies, preside at baptisms and weddings, and lead in charitable roles. But only celibate priests can say Mass and perform the big sacraments of consecrating the Eucharist, hearing confessions, and absolving sins.

"I'm not so interested in preaching," my father continues. "I'd like to bring the Gospel into the workplace. I have an idea for getting ex-cons into the business sector."

"Wow, Dad, I never knew that you . . . *thought* much about that kind of thing."

"The Lord has been calling me to it." He smiles. "What do you think?"

"I have to take a leak."

I hurry to the bathroom and stand pissing, feeling sucker punched, staring into the urinal.

The urinal stares back and says, *Your father is stronger than you.*

Fuck you, I think. *Fuck you, German urinal.*

He is, insists the urinal. *He's obeying the promptings of his faith and he'll be a great deacon. Meanwhile, you're a coward. You think every day about becoming a priest but you're not doing squat about it except talking to a urinal.*

I spit into the urinal. *Why can't I have my fairy-tale year and deal with the priesthood calling later? Why does every last fucking thing have to make me think of it, and why does my father have to be a deacon now so that I'll think of it even more? My life isn't a competition between me and my father!*

Well, says the urinal, *your life* is *a competition between you and the strongest version of yourself, the version God wants you to become. And that strongest version of you lies on the dark path, in the solitary contemplation of—*

"Shut up," I beg my own mind in a whisper. "I'm in love with Mara, not with God, so just please, please shut up."

I wash my hands and go back out to my father.

"Well, what do you think, David?"

"Um, it . . . it all sounds great, Dad."

GERMAN UNIVERSITIES have almost three months off between winter and summer semesters, so on Valentine's Day, 1990, I take a train to Florence to spend a month with Mara, which will be followed by a month of backpacking with Graham.

Florence is pretty, but I care only about Mara. Each night she and I make dinner in her apartment. Her friend Reston (another Hoya studying abroad) usually comes over, too. Reston boils pasta to a perfect al dente, while Mara and I make sauce. Often it's merely *aglio e olio*, just garlic and olive oil, but we get it down to a science. One night toward the end of my visit Mara pours olive oil into the frying pan and heats it, and after cutting the garlic finely I slide the minced-up cloves off the chopping blade, into the pan. We watch the white garlic specks roil in the oil.

Mara points to them. "Are they suffering?"

I put on a Darth Vader voice. "It is their destiny."

She laughs her murmuring laugh. The kitchen fills with the fruity smell of the oil and pungent garlic and Reston is singing "Don't Dream It's Over" and he strains the pasta and we eat. After dinner Reston goes home, and Mara brings out a bottle of Badedas, a European bath bodywash the color green of B-movie Martian goo.

"Smell this, Max. You'll love it."

She opens the bottle. It has horse chestnut extract in it, and we stand in the kitchen, inhaling like we're doing whip-its. Then we get in the tub and wash our bodies and hair with the Badedas and we look electric green from head to toe.

"You're an alien," she tells me.

"So are you."

We go to bed. I'm still cleaving to my no-actual-intercourse rule, but I have other ways to make Mara come, and I love to cause and witness and cheer the peaking powers of her body. Afterward, we lie in each other's arms.

"David . . ."

I somehow know what's coming next.

"You have to start making love to me again. Having full-on sex with me. Please, you have to. Sometime soon. I just . . ."

"I understand," I say.

"I can't help wanting all of you. That's how this is supposed to *work*. I want to raise your babies. Not yet, you know that, but . . . I just need all of you. I *miss* all of you. And what we do now, orgasms are great, but it's not enough . . . it makes me feel . . ."

She sighs. She sounds tired, ground down in a deep part of herself. "I've even tried going to church about this. I've tried praying to your God."

This floors me. "You've tried praying?"

"Yes. But . . ." Her voice gets small. Possibly angry. "I didn't hear anything."

"Mara, you don't have to pray. Don't ever think that I think that you have to."

"David . . . please, we need to start fucking again. Sometime soon. Maybe by the time I come to Tübingen this summer? I've been trying to meet you halfway, honey, but . . ."

I nod into her neck. I nod because I understand, not because I know what I'll do. Later, after Mara is asleep, I call my mother from Mara's apartment phone, which is in the kitchen and out of earshot of the bedroom.

My mother is surprised to hear from me. Usually we schedule our calls. She asks if everything's all right. I say that it is.

"Hmm," she says. "What'd you have for dinner?"

My mother never believes that I'm okay unless I've recently dined. I once heard her tell someone that I eat as much as a horse and then I eat the horse.

"I had *aglio e olio*," I say.

"Stop showing off."

"I had pasta."

She is quiet. I listen to the international clicks on the line.

"Mom . . . you know all about Dad's deaconate stuff?"

"Of course."

I nod and stare around Mara's kitchen. It is a true Italian kitchen with bottles of Chianti on the table next to a bowl full of *pepperoncini* and an Italian newspaper open to an article about some soccer game. This afternoon Mara sat on the kitchen floor reading that article in just her underwear and a T-shirt of mine while spooning up from a bowl a snack of white beans with raw garlic and juice from fresh lemons. I think of my family's kitchen back home, the room my mother is in right now. She is a first-rate cook and baker. She makes unrivaled Rice Krispie brownies, not with marshmallows, but with German sweet chocolate and butterscotch. Neither of my parents has ever sat nor will ever sit on a floor in their underwear while munching garlic and beans. More things in that experience would be too raw for them than just the garlic.

"Mom . . . how'd you know that Dad was the one?"

"Uh-oh," says my mother. "David, you're only twenty."

"You were only twenty-two when you got married!"

She sighs. "I knew your father was the one because I would have been fine without him."

"That doesn't sound very romantic."

"Well, it is. I would've been fine without him, but I knew that life with him was what I wanted and that it would be wonderful. I *chose* it. I was free, and it was the right thing to do with my freedom." She pauses. "Did you have meat with the pasta?"

"No."

"You don't do well without meat. Next time have some meat."

"Okay."

There is more I want to ask her. But I can see the conversation in my imagination:

ME: Mom, should I be a priest or should I resume screwing Mara's brains out nightly?

MY MOM: (*No dialogue. Horrified, she passes out. A pan of butterscotch chocolate Rice Krispie brownies falls from her hand.*)

So I ask no more questions. We say that we miss and love each other and then we hang up.

A FEW DAYS LATER I catch a train up to Vienna to meet Graham and we launch a spring trip we've been planning. Our first stop is Prague. Its famous castle is sprawling and stately. The exchange rate is enough of a steal that at dinner our first night I pay just two American dollars for a whole roasted duck and a bottle of Riesling. I'm so happy that Dam-and-Grave are reunited that after finishing, I order the whole meal again. Graham keeps pace, putting away two plates of venison and two bottles of cabernet.

Next is a train trip to Budapest, and while we're on board

Graham discovers that I carry a rosary in the front pocket of my jeans. He's told me several times that he doesn't believe in God, and he looks stunned now, or betrayed, and he asks me questions. When it's clear to him that I actually use the rosary regularly, he harrumphs.

"Wait . . . you haven't ever prayed for *me*, have you?"

I lie. "Um, no."

"Don't you ever pray for me," he threatens. "I mean it, Schick."

He has dark moods and motivations sometimes. One reason we stay friends is because when he gets a certain glare in his eyes, I leave him be.

"Okay," I say.

Our goal is Greece. After Budapest, we get a train south but it stops at the border between Hungary and Yugoslavia. Intimidating soldiers in gray overcoats board and start yelling in Hungarian and looking at passports.

They order off the train all Americans and everyone who's not Hungarian or Yugoslavian. I'm in the train's bathroom, suffering chronic diarrhea, but even from the bathroom throne I can see out the window a concrete building into which all American passengers are being herded. A knock comes on the door and I hear Graham.

"Hey, come on out, man, there's a guard here. He needs to see our passports and they're in there with you in your rucksack. I think we're getting booted."

"I can't come out," I grunt.

"He can't come out," Graham tells the guard. He tries to explain my plight in German.

"Him, name." The guard raps the door, speaks broken English. "Him, in there, name . . . what is?"

"You don't speak any German?" Graham asks.

"No." The guard bangs on the door again. "Him name . . . what is?"

I'm not sure why Graham says what he says next. I think he knows that I'm stressed about Mara. In any case he tells the guard, "His name is Delphin. Dell-fain."

The guard raps the door. "Delphin in there, you come out."

I'm still indisposed, but I start laughing, hard. It gets up under my ribs.

"Delphin? You, out, now!"

I clench my teeth and hold back howls. The guard keeps calling me a dolphin. He opens the door and juts his head in. He's glaring, then his hand flies up to cover his nose.

"Oh, *Delphin*," he says.

In hysterics, I slap the wall. As the guard ducks out, I can tell from his face that he won't haul me off the toilet. When the train continues south minutes later, Graham and I are the only Americans still on it.

We stop in Belgrade, Yugoslavia, for one night. There are visible bits of soot in the air from some factory or another, and when I sneeze into a white Kleenex, it turns black. We order food at a local restaurant and get served some cooked intestines that, as near as we can tell, are stuffed with other cooked intestines. Feeling like very ugly Americans, we end up eating dinner instead at a McDonald's, where an old woman patron with kind eyes and zero teeth tries to sell me playing cards featuring pornographic pictures of naked gymnasts. Belgrade is not for us.

We end up in Matala, on the south shore of the island of Crete. There are white cave-pocked cliffs. It is fifty degrees out at best. It's early April and the season doesn't start until May, and Graham and I are the only tourists in town. We sit shirtless on beaches of tiny round stones, shivering, indignant that the sun won't warm us and that we're not getting the dream vacation which we planned. Finally we leave Crete for Ios.

I've arranged for us to meet up on Ios with Mara and two Alabama Boys (who are studying abroad as well) and their girlfriends. The Alabama Boys and their sweethearts arrive first, and while they settle at the hostel, I wait on the dock for the day's last ferry. It arrives with a searing orange sunset at its back. Mara is on the ferry deck and I can tell it's her just by her silhouette.

"Maaax!" She bounds down the gangplank into my arms like a soldier's wife.

I've splurged to get us the nicest hostel room, a private one with a big bed. At a local restaurant we and all our friends have a giant laugh-fest of a meal that lasts until midnight, and I get the DJ to play "Stir It Up," my and Mara's favorite Bob Marley song. But later as Graham is singing Sinatra and making the room whoop, Mara starts crying. She's watching an Alabama

Boy and his girlfriend kiss and I know that she's seeing in them some unassailable oneness, some deep agreement of being. She goes out onto the terrace and I follow.

"Mara," I say. "Mar." It's a nickname that I use only in emergencies. I put my arms around her while she looks at the ocean.

"You're upset about the Medjugorje plan, right?" I say. "Look, let's just bag it."

Mara has agreed that after Ios, she and I will break off from the others and travel to Medjugorje, the Yugoslav village where the Virgin Mary has allegedly appeared. I have doubts about the place, but I've longed to see it.

"We're not bagging it," Mara insists, wiping her eyes. "It's important to you . . . so it's important to me."

FROM IOS, she and I take the ferry to Athens. We take a train to Yugoslavia and then get up into the mountains to Medjugorje by bus. The terrain is free of vegetation. Among the dirt and rocks is a church, and pilgrims visit a hillside spot where visitations have allegedly happened. We see candles and crucifixes around a shrine. Most of the pilgrims are middle-aged Americans in windbreakers. I arrange for Mara and me to piggyback onto a tour group as they meet the eldest visionary.

She is a young woman named Vicka, and speaking through a translator she answers questions. I ask Vicka what she or for that matter Mary feels about the world's many religions and the bitter divides among them. Once she understands my question Vicka smiles and speaks to the translator.

"Vicka says," the translator tells me, "that there is only one God."

Later in the day we go to the nearby seaside town of Dubrovnik. While Mara goes off to take photographs I duck into a church. There's an American tour group celebrating Mass. They've just been to Medjugorje and are soon to fly home. Several people in the group keep glancing at one woman among them. She is around fifty, and the others nudge her to talk. She shakes her head until the group's priest asks if she'll please tell the story just one more time. She stands.

She says that a few years ago she had malignant tumors in her head—a large one at the base of her brain, and a smaller one on the left side—and that surgeons removed them. She convalesced, losing her hair and lots of weight. She eventually came through it, but she had a paralyzing fear that the tumors would come back.

Then in Medjugorje she was on the shrine hill during a prayer ceremony. Afterward a man came up to her. He was Latvian and spoke no English, and he could communicate only via his friend, who translated. He told the woman that during the ceremony he'd been in the crowd below her. He said that he'd seen two glowing images on her head, one larger one near the base of her skull and a smaller one on her head's left side. He said that they were faces shining in her dark hair. He said that he believed he'd seen the face of Christ.

"So I just know now that they . . ." The woman gestures at her own bowed head. "They're gone for good. I'll die someday, but not from them."

When the Mass ends I hurry to the city's castle ramparts where Mara and I agreed to meet. She's sitting on a giant black ship's anchor.

"What happened?" she asks. "You look keyed up."

"There was a woman at church . . ." I try to tell the story, but it comes out puny and false.

"Did you believe her?"

"I don't know."

Mara squeezes my hand, but looks off at some clouds. She knows that whether or not I believe the story, I want to, whereas she requires only the day and the sky and Dubrovnik and me.

BACK IN TÜBINGEN I will myself not to fret about Mara's upcoming July visit. For a while I distract myself, because Tübingen is summer-beautiful. Each morning there is bright dew on the lawns around Waldhäuser Ost. The Neckar River is rapid with bubbling mountain runoff and every day is sunny. Graham and I have classes all day on Tuesdays and Wednesdays, but then, incredibly, a five-day weekend each week. We throw Frisbees and cook dinners with Audrey and Nicole.

And then Mara arrives. Her first night in town there's a giant party in a dorm called Studo. Beer flows and there's no air-conditioning and the dance floor is a packed, bouncing fire hazard. Mara's wearing a peasant-green dress and purple, pottery-made earrings I bought her and we dance and dance.

When "Love Shack" comes on, we tug each other down a hall. Clattering into an empty, echoing women's shower room, we sneak into a shower stall, kissing and groping. I hike up her dress and pull off her underwear and she leans back against the wall. I'm hard and ready and Mara's eyes on mine are warm with urging. I tell her that I love her.

I kiss her neck while the B-52s tell me to Just Fuck This Girl Already.

My arms are wrapped around her. My cock stays on the brink, uncommitted.

Go on, I tell myself. *This is what lovers do!*

I kiss her shoulders and neck. We stand there, with me wavering. I wish, God how I wish, that I were anyone but me, that I could believe anything but what I do. When Mara finally sighs, it's a death knell. I slump against the wall, my cheeks red-hot and emasculated.

"David, the fact that you can't . . . the fact that you *won't* . . . it makes me feel like I disgust you."

I taste something acidic in my mouth. I stand there naked, sorry. "Mara, please. Mar."

She turns away and leans her temple to the tile wall, hanging her head, letting gravity do what it does to her hair. I see the river-rapids scar on her neck, vulnerable and crooked. I reach out and touch it.

"Help," I say, like I have a thousand times. "I'm a ship caught in these river rapids. Somebody help."

Mara whirls around, her eyes wide and afraid and she hugs me hard. "What's happening, honey?" she cries out. "What're we *doing*?"

Ending, I think.

Just weeks later we're back at Georgetown. Mara and I break up and she starts dating and sleeping with a Hawaiian guy named Akoni, and my fairy tale is done.

Chapter Five

A MONTH LATER, on an October morning of my senior year,
I sit in the office of Father Roy Tillermacher and tell him that
I want to become a Jesuit priest.

An hour beforehand I paced around on Copley Lawn, trading telepathies with inanimate objects.

I'm afraid, I told a stone wall.

You're ready, the wall assured me. *Take the leap. You'll still
be you once you're a priest. Just a stronger you.*

I'll be lonely, I thought toward the John Carroll statue.

God's grace will get you through, the statue said.

Finally I closed my eyes. *All right, Lord. I love You. I'm all
Yours.*

Father Tillermacher has an office just a couple buildings
away from the Jesuit Residence, known as the Jez-Rez. The Jez-
Rez is a red-brick building containing Jesuit apartments and

the white-linen Jesuit dining hall, which students can visit only with a priest.

I'm confiding my vocation in Father Tillermacher rather than Father Prince. I still love Father Prince's Masses, but he scares me. He never swears or even gossips, and he's so emaciated that it looks like God took a knife to the guy and whittled him down. I love playing Ultimate Frisbee too much to want to look like that. I want to be strong. A warrior priest!

Father Tillermacher is more approachable. He's originally from South Dakota and has muscles and says "fuck" sometimes. As I sit with him, he asks me why I want to be a priest.

"I can't stop thinking about it. I feel like God is inviting me to do it for Him and I don't think I can live with myself if I say no. And because of . . ."

"Yes?"

The clock in his office tings and tongs.

Because of the dark path, I think. *It's where I come from and it's where I'm headed and it makes no sense to live on it alone, but I have to. I have to empty my life and go there and worship God from there.*

"David?" asks Father Tillermacher. "You were saying?"

I clam up. I don't talk about the path with anyone. "I can't think of anything gutsier that I could do."

Father Tillermacher raises his eyebrows. He asks if he can give me some Scripture passages to read and pray over with regard to my feelings. I agree. He asks if I've discussed my vocation with anyone else. I say no.

"Is this something your parents encouraged you towards? Giving a son to the priesthood can be a great honor for parents, but it can also be a pressure that they place on—"

"They've never suggested it."

"You came to this on your own?"

I nod.

"And it's just between you and me, for now?"

"Yes, please," I say. "For now."

I LIVE IN a house off campus with five other senior guys: the Alabama Boys (they're now a force of three—Mason, Daniel, and Austin—because Bob fell away somehow), and a painter and an actor. Our living room has ratty purple couches. The Alabama Boys and the painter have girlfriends, so any one of these couples can usually be found on the couches. On the walls are oil-on-canvas works that the painter made, inspired by notes we've left around the house. My favorite says WHO DRANK MY FUCKING MILK?

I get home one evening to find Mason standing on one couch, rapping from memory the song "My Hooptie" by Sir Mix-A-Lot. Mason's girlfriend and the other Boys sit on the opposite couch, laughing. Cross-legged on the floor is Daphne Lowell, a pretty brunette from Vermont who shares a dorm room with Mason's girlfriend.

"Hey, cannibal!" Mason yells as I come in. "Get in here!"

I join the others. Mason stands astride the couch, glaring

down at me. "I saw you today, going into that secret dining hall with What's-His-Face."

"Father Tillermacher," I say.

Mason folds his arms. "What goes on in that place, Schick? Isn't it suspicious that I, a lapsed Baptist, don't get invited, but you get the inner sanctum buffet?"

"Here we go." Austin sighs. He and the others are used to watching me and Mason go at it.

I say, "Father Tillermacher's a really good guy."

"They're *grooming* you, Schick!" Mason stomps his foot. "The Jesuits are fucking recruiting you and I won't let it happen."

Daphne smiles to herself. Besides being beautiful and smart, she's the only other person in the room who was raised Catholic and still goes to Mass. She gets a kick out of it when Mason goes apeshit on me. Also her voice and laugh are wonderful and she might be my wife.

"Mason," I say, "why is it so bad if I have a harmless lunch with—"

"*It's not harmless!* Those priests are fucking sneaky and you're my buddy!" He paces on the couch. "You're not like them, dammit, you're like *us*!" He stabs his finger around at our friends. "You can't be a Jesuit, Schick. Don't beat your head against that two-thousand-year-old wall. I want you to be free!"

I point a finger at him, too. "You want me to be free the way a Bolshevik wants a man to be free. Meaning, as long as I bail on believing in God and thinking that maybe that requires something of me . . . as long as I bail on all that, *then* I'm free."

He looks like he'll leap down and punch me.

"Guys, enough," says Austin.

Mason unclenches his fists. "Schick. If you become a priest—You. Will. Be. Miserable." He storms off to his room.

A few weeks later Mara invites me to her apartment for dinner with her and Akoni, her Hawaiian boyfriend. All fall she's been inviting me to do things, but I've declined. I can still smell the skin over her ribs just by thinking of her, and I've jolted awake many nights after moving my lips toward what my sleeping body still trusts will be the nape of her neck beside me. This makes me sure that any post-breakup time spent with her will be torture, but Mara keeps calling me, insisting that we're friends who can stay close. Maybe she just wants to see if I'm okay. Finally, stupidly, I agree to dinner.

Mara says on the phone that we'll be having pasta *aglio e olio*, our old favorite. I arrive at her apartment with a bottle of Chianti. Mara greets me at the door, looking killer good in a green sweater and black stretch pants. Behind her stands a tall, beefy, black-haired guy who looks like maybe his ancestors sacrificed virgins in volcanoes. Mara and I hug awkwardly. She holds her hand out, indicating the Polynesian elephant in the room.

"Dave, have you met Akoni before? Akoni, Dave. Okay, Dave, you're on garlic duty, you're the pro at that, and I'll be on oil and pasta, and Akoni, you pour wine."

We go to our stations, do our jobs. The meal goes fine until dessert, by which point Akoni is a bit drunk and stroking Mara's hair and sneering at me. I focus on my dessert, a dish of vanilla ice cream with crushed Skor bars. Mara and I ate this regularly sophomore year and I know that she's served it now to make me comfortable.

"So, Dave," says Akoni, "you're pretty Catholic, yes?"

Mara clears her throat. "Don't ask him about that, please."

I say, "I guess I am."

Akoni keeps stroking Mara's hair. They're sitting across from me. His hand keeps a lazy rhythm on her, up and down, then burrows into her hair to where her river-rapids scar lies.

Don't touch that scar, I think toward his hand. *It's hers and mine.*

"I hear that you take the Catholic stuff really seriously." His sneer hasn't quit. "Like, you don't even believe in having full premarital sex."

Mara slams her spoon down. "What did I say?! Don't ask him about that!"

"This has been wonderful." I leave. Mara follows and catches me on the landing outside. She holds my arm.

"I'm sorry," she whispers.

"What'd you think would happen? He's a guy, I'm a guy . . ."

"He's heard so much about you from me that this is hard for him."

This is hard for him? "I should go."

"David—I saw you yesterday talking to that cute Asian girl from the nursing school."

I have sweat behind my knees. I wonder if a sharpened Skor bar could be stabbed through Akoni's eyeball, into his brain.

"She seems great. You were making her laugh, and Reston tells me he's seen her going to Mass, so she probably believes the same things that—"

"Mara, don't."

"Ask her out, honey." She squeezes my wrist. "Please, I need you to be happy. Call her, okay?"

We say a tense good-night. I go to the campus pub and drink and dance. "Tenderness" by General Public plays, and I move with the beat, stomping my feet on Akoni's face, which is really just the dance floor. Swaying couples around me look pissed, but I keep it up. "She Drives Me Crazy" by Fine Young Cannibals comes on and I morph to the beat. My father's father was a solo flyer on dance floors, too. He, Grampa Joe the farmer, would escort my grandmother to hoedowns in barns. She'd head home early, but he'd stay and whirl in the sawdust till the fiddlers quit.

I stumble home from the pub at two a.m., sweaty and chilly and weaving along the Reservoir Road sidewalk. The wind stings. I stare at trees and shadows.

One sentence, Lord, I pray. *Just talk to me once. Tell me I'm moving in the right direction.*

I hear nothing. The wind whips. My armpits are raw with

sweat. When I get home I collapse in my clothes on my bed. The room spins. A knock comes on my door.

"Who's there?" I croak.

"The Bolshevik." Mason lets himself in. I aim my face at the wall, not looking at him. He pulls off my shoes and tosses them, then sits on the floor near my head.

"Are you drunk, Schick?"

"Yes."

I'm still facing away from him.

"So . . . I guess dinner went well."

I tell him what Akoni said.

"Schick, you know that Mara's probably still in love with you, right? And that you're definitely still in love with her?"

I nod. Mason sighs. My eyes adjust to the dark and I see on my wall the things I've hung there, a crucifix, and a poster for the vampire film *The Hunger*. I wonder why people my age have to put shit all over their walls that says *This is who I am!*

Mason says, "Can you tell me again why you stopped fucking Mara? You're afraid of knocking her up? You're afraid of abortion?"

I close my eyes. "That's part of it. But mostly . . ." I pause. "You think I'm a simpleminded papist. Why do you care?"

"I'm your buddy."

The spins get to me and I open my eyes. On my movie poster of *The Hunger*, standing over a corpse, is David Bowie in a tailored dark suit and sunglasses. Also crouching over the corpse, licking blood from her lips, is a sexy Catherine Deneuve.

"I can't fully fuck someone I'm not married to," I say to the wall. "It taps a part of me meant only for God. If I married Mara, then that part of me would *become* fully meant for her, with God's approval, and I could make love to her completely. Please don't tease me about all this tonight."

"I'm not." He's quiet for a minute. "So today you had that Pixies song 'Debaser' blaring in here and you were singing it crazy loud."

"Sorry."

"You sing it a lot. Tell me why you're so into it."

"Mace..."

"Just tell me."

I think about it. I turn to face him. "Even though it mentions creepy stuff like sliced eyeballs, the song isn't creepy, it's just fast and great. And I love how Black Francis and Kim Deal sing together. It's fucked-up but perfect."

Mason is nodding agreement.

I say, "I wish I could sing with someone like that. Or write something like that."

"News flash, buddy. We're both going to grow up to be debasers and that's a good thing." He stands. "Go to sleep."

He leaves and closes the door.

A MONTH LATER I'm in Father Tillermacher's office. We've discussed some Scripture passages and now he's showing me pictures of Jesuit novitiate houses around the United States.

For a man to enter the Jesuits, he has to apply to a Jesuit province and upon acceptance begin novitiate training, living in community with other novices, studying, ministering in charity, and firming up his commitments to poverty, chastity, and obedience. Father Tillermacher is urging me to apply to the New York province since I'm a native New Yorker.

"And how was your Agape retreat?" he asks.

Last weekend I attended a campus ministry retreat in the Virginia mountains. Unlike my silent retreat freshman year, which was about a personal relationship with God, this retreat was social, focused on community. Thirty Georgetown undergrads attended. There were spiritual discussions, but also touch-football games and skits.

"It was pretty good."

"You're lying," says Father Tillermacher.

"It was somewhat dorky."

"Why?"

On the retreat I met many wonderful people who weren't dorky. But somehow there was dorkiness in the air. "Someone kept playing 'Shower the People' on guitar and people sang along."

"So?" Father Tillermacher looks like he's waiting for me to display something a Jesuit novice will need, something like insight.

I spill what I feel is the truth. "'Shower the People' sucks. Jesus never showered the people. He healed them and scared them. He was gritty and dangerous and never a dork. Agape was dorky. It was too . . ." I'm not sure of the word. Too spiffy. Too upbeat. Too bubbly-safe. "I don't think I'm above a retreat like that, but when I was on it I couldn't feel God's danger. I couldn't find the Bottom, the . . . the dark of God."

This is as close as I've ever gotten to talking about the dark path with anyone. I fidget my hands. Father Tillermacher has a complicated light in his eyes. Is he impressed? Concerned?

"David, do you know the passage in Matthew that reads 'From the days of John the Baptist until now the kingdom of heaven suffers violence, and violent men take it by force'?"

"Yes."

"What do you think it means?"

"That God and His followers are surrounded by conflict. And if you want to know God, you might have to relish that. You might have to battle and claim a place in His company."

Father Tillermacher studies me. "And that's what you want to be? A violent man in that sense? A man fighting to find— I'll use your phrase—God's danger and darkness?"

"Yes."

"Hmm."

"Why 'hmm'?"

"If you look hard enough for that kind of fight, God just might give it to you."

I sense that he's warning me seriously, but I want to be accepted by his club. I try some levity. "Do you think the Jesuits will want a fight-picking punk like me?"

He smiles, letting down his guard. "I think we already do."

He gives me a hug, which has become our custom, and I leave.

I AM OBSESSED with short stories lately. Each evening I go to Lauinger Library and sit in a big cushioned chair and lose myself in the short stories of Bernard MacLaverty, Shirley Jackson, Flannery O'Connor. Like poetry and Shakespeare have rocked me in the past, short fiction is dazzling me now. I read over and over two short stories in particular—"Goodbye, My Brother" by John Cheever and "Where Are You Going, Where Have You Been?" by Joyce Carol Oates. These stories make me feel like I'm plugged into a secret electrical current that runs under the surface of life. They're so damned good that they make me want to throw a thousand punches or fuck a thousand girls or kiss the sun.

I can't understand why, but when I read them, I feel carried far outside myself and simultaneously driven deeper into myself. Only praying, running, and sex with Mara have ever made me feel that way. I'm jealous of these stories . . . I want to have written them. I want and need to get at truth the way that they do. I feel like God must be entertained or moved by these stories, and I feel like they're the answer to something dire.

Something is shifting inside me as a student of the world. I've begun thinking that the world's leaders—the people I've studied for years in my Foreign Service program—need to shut the fuck up about themselves and their agendas and geopolitical this and national sovereignty that. Maybe if everyone could just read more American Cheever and drink more Italian Chianti and eat more German spaetzle and try whatever sexual positions the French are inventing lately, we'd all have more fun and we wouldn't get so ripshit defensive with each other. I have no fully evolved theories about all this, just suspicions. And my suspicions make me want to write fiction. If there is truth in John Cheever's and Joyce Carol Oates's work, then God is in that work, too. And priests are committed to all facets of the truth, I tell myself. I decide that I will be a priest who writes fiction. And plays Ultimate Frisbee. And says "fuck" sometimes.

So throughout the fall I start writing my own short stories, forgoing classwork to do so. Every night I make brilliant progress. Every morning, whatever I wrote the night before reads like utter shit and I throw it out. But I keep doing it. I get better.

As Christmas approaches, I write a special story, a semiautobiographical one. I write it for my father. It's clunky, but it ends with a young man at night on a dark path. As the young man stares into the shadows under some trees, the fireflies above the shadows swirl and form letters that say: *be a priest, be a priest, be a priest.*

One afternoon when I'm home over Christmas break, I ask my father to go into the kitchen. "I left you something on the table to read," I tell him.

My mother and sisters aren't home. I lurk in the living room while he reads. Soon he joins me. He is holding my story and looking at it like it's a ticket to some miraculous place.

"David? Does this mean what I think it means?"

I nod. "You're the only one I want to know for now, Dad, but I'm going to be a priest. If the Jesuits will have me."

His cheeks pink up. He hugs me. "Oh, David. I'm so glad for you. Your mother and I . . . we've wondered . . ."

He sits on the couch. His eyes mist. And then suddenly, awfully, something in his facial expression falters, or falls away. I've never seen it happen before. It's as if there's some cave inside him, some haunted place I didn't know about, and for the first time I am seeing the entrance to it. My father starts crying. Hard. He looks agonized.

My muscles lock up in panic. He has never even teared up in front of me.

"Dad!" I sit, put my arms around him. "Dad, what's wrong?"

He's shaking. Then he tells me, in a rush. He's leaving General Motors, where he's worked for three decades. GM closed Rochester Products a while back and he's been commuting by car—on his dime—to Detroit for a year, spending weekends in Rochester with my mother and living in a Detroit motel on weeknights. I've known about his commute, but he says that the traveling isn't the problem.

He says that there's a certain powerful colleague who's making things impossible for him. "So I'm resigning. And I've got an idea for a company to start, and I'm pursuing the deaconate, but I . . . I just want to be a good man, David." He clings to me.

Still terrified, I pat his back. *Be stronger than me,* I beg him in my mind. *Please stop crying and be stronger than me, that's your job.*

He says, "I thought I was part of a good thing. And here now you're going to do the best of all things—"

"I'll do it for you," I blurt.

As he leans against my chest, I focus on the wild gray hairs and stray liver spots on the back of his neck. I listen as his breathing eventually eases. I'll give up anything to calm him and make him proud. Anything.

ALL WINTER I keep up my talks with Father Tillermacher as I prepare to tell my friends and family of my priesthood plans. I also keep writing short stories and on a lark I apply to some master's programs in fiction, just to see if I get in. For me priesthood and creativity will intertwine. At McQuaid I admired a priest who wrote books and had a role in the film *The Exorcist*. He seemed to praise God through art and I decide that I'll do that, too. The Jesuits have room for all types, Mystics, Bodybuilders, Cut-Ups, everything. What they don't have yet is a Kick-Ass Author Priest who wins the National Book Award for fiction. That's where I will come in.

The priest who acted in *The Exorcist* was also a singer, and in February at Georgetown I try singing. I audition for the annual talent show, Cabaret. It's a night when a house band plays at a bar while students sing covers of rock songs. I make it past the first audition round by performing "Stray Cat Strut."

The final callback is in the campus pub one weeknight. Performers pack the place. The Alabama Boys show up to support me as I take the stage and launch into "Somebody" by Depeche Mode. I'm halfway through the song when the crowd shifts and I see Mara and Akoni sitting, drinking beers, listening, as he strokes her cheek. They look oddly good together, her with her long red hair and him with his black chop of a haircut. I stare at them. It takes cleared throats in the crowd for me to realize that the music's playing but I've stopped singing. Mara's mouth opens with what looks like concern for me, but although I've practiced for days I can't remember more lyrics.

Crimson, I hop offstage and leave the pub. Mara follows me, alone. She catches up with me in the Student Union hall.

"You were doing great," she says. "What happened?"

I look off at the posters outside the pub, advertising guitar lessons, Spanish language lessons, fencing lessons. Everybody has lessons to offer.

"You know what happened."

We look at each other. Mara shakes her head, as if to deny any tension between us. "Can't we just be friends, honey?"

"Mara, you can't call me 'honey' anymore. I—I can't—" *I can't live life when you're around. I can't pretend that I don't crave and miss every inch of you. I've made a choice about my future and you're fucking it up by continuing to exist.*

"Just go be with Akoni," I say and I leave.

ON AN APRIL DAY I sit praying with Father Tillermacher in the living room of his on-campus apartment. We've prayed like this before, since Georgetown students often visit priests in their living quarters (each dorm has one live-in priest so students can ask for spiritual guidance).

Outside, the cherry trees are in bloom. In a few minutes I'll be on Copley Lawn, playing Ultimate with Graham. But right now I'm thanking God for the path that I feel strengthening in me. I plan to contact the New York Province of the Society of Jesus—the Jesuits' technical name—within the month to start my application.

Father Tillermacher and I each say things that we're grateful for, and we make sure to name each other.

"I'll be proud and excited," he says, "when you become my brother Jesuit."

"I will, too."

We stand and give each other our customary parting hug.

Then, while he's hugging me, he squeezes my right ass cheek in his left fist and holds on for ten seconds past what would be an acceptable football-field or locker-room ass slap from a coach to a player.

Wait, I think. *What's this, wait, wait—*

As he holds my ass, I hear a rushing in my ears, like in a cartoon when a character freezes solid, *whoosh*, because ice wind is blasting him.

I break away, though not violently. Father Tillermacher hasn't attacked me. It is worse for having been a probing, secret handshake of a gesture: an invitation.

"Okay, 'bye," I say brightly, trying to sound normal.

I leave. On Copley Lawn I climb up into what some students call Uncle Treemus, a massive oak tree with thick branches. I sit on a high branch and don't move. In my mind I flip through every interaction I've ever had with Father Tillermacher. I look at the blocking and the dialogue, where he stood, where I stood, what he said, what I said. There's a faint noise in the air. It's my voice whispering *"Godfuckingdammit, godfuckingdammit."*

Looking back, I can't find suggestiveness in his behavior on any prior day. And I know that there won't be more unless I ask. Something quietly unambiguous has been left in my court.

"Schickler? What the hell are you doing up there?"

I look down. Graham is at the base of the tree, holding two Frisbees. In Tübingen we threw these same disks each afternoon. When we play Ultimate, each of us can bullet the Frisbee through dozens of opponents' waving arms and bull's-eye the disk into the other guy's hands. It's our closest connection.

"Time to throw, man. There's like twenty other chumps waiting for us to chew them up and spit them out."

I don't answer. Graham climbs up beside me.

"What's the problem, Schick? Too busy to throw with your best heathen buddy?"

He clonks my head with a disk. When I still don't speak, his face gets serious. "Hey, for real, are you all right? Did you get into something with somebody?"

He glares around the base of the tree, looking for potential offenders. He is a loyal, impulsive friend. If I tell him what happened, he will go rip the priest's lungs out.

"Don't worry about it," I say quickly. "It's just SWM."

Graham groans. SWM is our code for Shit With Mara. If I show up at Graham's off-campus house at night and say "SWM" he gets us a couple Anchor Steams and we sit on his lawn, drinking, not needing to talk.

"Schickler," he says now, "no moping about pussy today. The sun is shining and it's time to throw."

I stare at the sky. It's not like I haven't heard of priests making moves on young people. There was a priest in the drama program at McQuaid who had to "go away for a while" because he'd been caught sharing "hugs" with several girls from our sister high school, Our Lady of Mercy, during rehearsals for a McQuaid-and-Mercy spring musical. And here at Georgetown there's a handsome, witty priest who's rumored to be an actively gay regular on the D.C. nightclub circuit. But stories like that have always been around, and whether they've been cautionary whispers or jokes, they've been peripheral to me. Until now. Godfuckingdammit.

"Hey." Graham nudges me. "If you don't get off this fucking branch, I'll shove you off it."

Inside I'm still jarred. But I'm grateful for Graham and I hop down out of the tree and he does too and we run out onto the lawn to chew up chumps and spit them out.

Chapter Six

I GET ACCEPTED into the Creative Writing Program at Columbia University and in August I move to New York City. Inside, I remain shaken. My plans to apply immediately to the Jesuits are stalled.

I yell at Father Tillermacher in my mind. *THERE'S NO FUCKING ON THE PATH!*

I thought sacrificing sex and Mara had cleared my way for a priestly, contemplative life. Now contemplative life has literally grabbed my ass and I can't reconcile it. By mail I keep in guarded touch with Father Tillermacher, never bringing up what happened. I still know that I'll end up an Artistic Priest, but I confide to my father—without saying what happened— that I need some time before joining the Jesuits.

I lecture myself. *You were talking too much with one man*

behind closed doors. You should've been out in the world, acting, building up what you can bring to the Jesuits, what you can do for God.

Thinking this way, I decide that there will be a new fork on my path toward full priesthood. Saint Paul says that if we are richly gifted in any one way, we should use that gift for the building up of the greater assembly, the wider community. Well, Columbia MFA Admissions seems to feel that I have a gift for writing. So I've moved here not only so that I can write fiction for God, but so that I can teach others to write well, too. All of this will make me a better Father Schickler someday, I tell myself.

This new MO of mine lands me one September day in the Columbia Learning Center, a tutoring facility in Lewisohn, a building that sits along Broadway. I've been hired to tutor students in writing during one-on-one sessions. On this day I work with an Israeli exchange student, and when we're done I check the sign-up sheet. Written in my next time slot is the name Melvin Duggles. I look around the center.

"Is there a Melvin Duggles?"

"Psst," hisses a voice. "Over here."

The two large ficus plants in the corner are whispering to me. I approach and see a human figure crouched behind them.

"Melvin?"

"It's a game," says the figure. "You have to find me."

"I found you. We're talking."

He emerges from behind the plants, grinning shyly or wickedly, I can't tell which. He looks about my age with bulging, froggy eyes and a tattered cap pulled down over greasy black hair. He is wearing a hooded gray sweatshirt that features a flamingo standing on it. The sweatshirt is also covered with huge coffee stains.

When the girl at the check-in desk sees who I'm talking to, she waves me over. "Most tutors won't work with him," she warns.

I look Melvin over. He has a picked-last-on-the-playground air about him, but I tell myself that the Lord cares for fringe individuals, so I should, too.

I think, *Be priestly, Schickler. Help the greater assembly. Help Melvin.*

Melvin and I sit at a table and he shows me a paragraph he's working on for his English class. His assignment is to describe a room and a person entering it, and he's been told to "set a mood via description." As I read, Melvin watches me intently.

"I like you," he says. "I know you'll help my writing. And looks-wise, you have a real Mel Gibson thing going on."

His paragraph is single-spaced in caps and bold type. It reads:

THE MAN WALKED DOWN INTO THE
BASEMINT, WHICH WAS DRAK AND

DICKENSIAN. ALSO THERE WAS A BAT IN BASEMINT AND THE BAT WAS ALSO DICK-ENSIAN. THE MAN DINT HAVE A NAME BUT HE WAS DICKENSIAN. PHANTASMAGORIA. THE MAN DINT LIKE THE BAT, 'AH' YELLED THE MAN, HE STEPPED ON BAT, THE BASE-MINT WAS IN WALES.

My first ungenerous thought is to wonder how the fuck Melvin Duggles ever got into Columbia. I ask him questions. It turns out that he's a gifted math major, but he needs to pass English Logic and Rhetoric to graduate and he failed it last year. As we talk I try to ignore his scent. He smells half soapy and half sour, like a hospital floor scrubbed with too weak a detergent.

Get past it, I tell myself. *Help the community*.

"We'll handle grammar later, Melvin," I say. "First let's talk about diction. You're trying to set a spooky mood in this piece, but—"

"You're right!" Melvin crows. "Halloween is coming up and I want this essay to be creepy. And Dickensian."

"Okay. But ironically *Dickensian* isn't a very Dickensian word. For example . . . which word sounds more powerful to you, *stab* or *violent*?"

Melvin blinks at me with his owlish eyes. "You're saying the guy should stab the bat instead of stepping on it?"

"What? No. It's just . . . you're trying to write a dark piece, but *phantasmagoria*, for example, isn't a dark-feeling word. It's scientific sounding."

Using a pen Melvin crosses out sentences on his paper and writes over them. "I'm just gonna do what you said and put in lots of stabbing."

"That's not what I said."

"No, you're right," says Melvin. "Life is violent. I'll tap into that."

MAYBE MELVIN READ my subconscious, because violence has been on my mind. Ever since Father Tillermacher got a fistful of my ass, I have felt fragile. I've been skinny since my cross-country days, but where I was once happy about that, I now feel defenseless. And increasingly fucking pissed. I love God but no one gets to just grab me. In the TV show *Kung Fu*, which I watched as a kid, Caine is a contemplative monk but also a le-thal motherfucker. I decide that I'll be like him. It will be an-other honing, a sharpening of myself, a priestly preparation.

I start taking Shotokan karate. I'm living on West 121st Street, across from Teacher's College, and the Teacher's Col-lege gym is where the Columbia Shotokan club trains two nights a week. Wearing a *gi*—a karate uniform—I learn punches, kicks, and blocks, and I do hundreds of push-ups on my knuckles on the hard gym floor. My knuckles hurt all the time from this and they're constantly bruised, but I can feel the bones in them getting denser, stronger.

One Monday night after karate I trudge across 121st Street to my apartment building, exhausted. My place is on the ground floor and through its open front windows I can see into my living room, where a crowd is having a party with my apartment mate, a law student named Tom Gumm. The university housing board threw us together randomly. Tom is a funny, smart Mormon guy from Salt Lake City, and every able-bodied local Mormon girl wants him as a husband.

I enter the apartment, go to the kitchen, get out my favorite stein and fill it with two bottles' worth of New Amsterdam beer. Then I head for the living room.

"Hi," I call to the group. I lift my stein in greeting and take a big swallow.

Everyone turns and stares at me and my beverage. It turns out that this isn't a party as I understand parties, but a Mormon tradition called Family Home Evening. It's a time, I learn later, for strengthening bonds of Christian love and maybe having a wholesome game or lesson (with no alcohol, tobacco, or caffeine allowed). As a leader of the singles in his Upper West Side ward, Tom will host Family Home Evening every other Monday this year.

The Mormons are quick to say that they're not offended by my beer, so I keep drinking and talk with three Mormon girls in a corner.

"Tom took me to see *Bob Roberts* last Saturday," says one. "The movie was cynical, but we had a nice dinner beforehand."

A second girl says, "Tom took me out for soul food in Harlem."

The third girl, Lurlene, is a quiet charmer who works at the concierge desk at a midtown hotel. She alone seems uncomfortable with the idea of openly discussing Tom, with whom she'll soon have her first date.

"How can you all like the same guy?" I ask. "If my sisters ever liked the same guy, they'd attack each other with machetes."

"Well," says the *Bob Roberts* girl, "a true union can't be based on that kind of jealousy and selfishness. You'll learn that, David, if you ever fall in love."

I stare into my beer, wondering what Mara Kincannon is doing at this moment. I've heard from Graham that she's working for a D.C. advertising agency and living with Akoni.

"I have. For two years I spent every second I could with a girl. But we broke up because I'm going to be . . ." I trail off, feeling stupid.

Lurlene touches my arm. "Hey, my friend didn't mean to pry. Right, Sarah?"

"Oh," says Sarah. "Right."

A guy sidles up and nudges me. "Bro . . . you look upset. Can I give you something?"

He pulls from his pocket a copy of the Book of Mormon and presses it into my palm. "Don't say anything. Just take it and put it aside and think about reading it someday and, for now, enjoy your alcohol."

"Okay," I say. I go to my room and stash the Book of Mormon in my boxer shorts drawer, feeling it would be rude to throw it out and misleading to display it. Then I go to the fridge for more beer.

As the weeks pass, Tom Gumm never tries to sell me on Mormonism. He lives his faith with calm and joy and I admire this, but I also admire the calm and joy with which he is dating virtually every unwed Mormon girl in Manhattan. He isn't fucking them or even getting naked and hooking up with them, yet he never seems frustrated. He eventually begins exclusively dating Lurlene the Mormon concierge. They come back from dates holding hands and cooing to each other.

One evening Tom and I are in midtown and we stop in to see Lurlene at the hotel where she works. She introduces me to another woman concierge there, Sabine, who is a couple years older than us and not Mormon. Sabine is funky hot, with long, black hair that she wears in a complicated braid, and she's a very slender six feet tall. She and Lurlene wear matching pink vest-and-skirt outfits that are apparently their uniforms. I admire Sabine as she helps a woman in a wheelchair find the elevator, then as she gives theater advice to a young couple with two small children.

"It's a wholesome production," she tells them, pointing to a brochure. "Family friendly."

Then she crouches and plays a version of peekaboo with the couple's shy daughter.

Standing tall in her shiny pink outfit, she looks like every gilded female archetype—the Prom Queen, the Princess, the Blushing Bride—that I'll soon have to leave behind for celibacy. Her cheeks glow each time she smiles.

I can't help flirting with Sabine and I end up getting her phone number. Back at my apartment I tell myself that it's okay to call her. Maybe I am inspired by Tom Gumm and Lurlene's budding romance. Maybe I want to punish Father Tillermacher. *I'll still be a priest soon, Father G*, I think, *but since you acted out and squeezed my ass, I get to act out and squeeze One Last Girl before I'm a Jesuit.* I think I'm basically looking to emulate Saint Augustine's famous mantra: *Dear Lord, make me chaste, but not yet.*

I go out with Sabine on Halloween night. She lives in Queens in a house with her aunt and uncle, and she takes the subway into Manhattan to meet me in Morningside Heights up by Columbia. She wears tight, all-black clothes and has a giant shoulder bag with her. She asks me to take her to see the horror flick *Candyman*. I oblige. After the film I take her to the Abbey Pub on West 105th.

"That movie was so fucking great," she says. We're at a table in a murky corner under a stained-glass window and we're drinking New Amsterdam ale. There's a lit candle between us and melted wax all over the table.

"I loved the decapitated Rottweiler," gushes Sabine. "I loved the bees crawling out of the killer's mouth and I loved the way he slashed the back of that woman's neck and she almost bled out, but not quite, and that way he could keep her alive and make her do his bidding. That was so fucking great."

When I first met her at the hotel, Sabine looked very poised and polite. But now, under the table, she's rubbing her bare foot against my inner thigh.

"I love this song!" She closes her eyes and nods with the music. "I fucking love Primus. Also Anthrax and Megadeth. Also Johnette Napolitano, the lead singer of Concrete Blonde, is the best female vocalist ever, so let's not even discuss it."

"Okay," I say.

She leans across the table and kisses my mouth. Her hair is out of its braid tonight and one of her long tresses brushes the candle and catches fire. Flame races up as if along a wick and without thinking I slap my hand hard against her head, snuffing the flame. She sits back in shock, and we both look at the puff of smoke beside her. The air smells burnt.

"Holy shit." She puts her hand to her scalp. "Did you *see* that?"

"I'm sorry. I didn't mean to hit you. I thought it would spread."

Her mouth hangs open in joy. "Don't apologize. That was so sexy! Right when I kissed you, *I caught on fucking fire*. Are you kidding me?"

"I really didn't mean to hit you."

Her eyes signal that she wants to be taken home, fast. We walk to my apartment. Tom Gumm and Lurlene are watching

TV in the living room, along with a Mormon whom Tom calls Sad Dog because the guy never has dates (Sad Dog has given me three Books of Mormon and they are all in my boxers drawer). Sabine says quick hellos, then pulls me into my bedroom and locks the door behind us.

"David, I am so totally horny for you right now. I feel really confident and horny."

I blush. I have no experience with dirty talk or really any talk during sexual encounters. Mara and I always just kissed and quietly willed our way forward.

"I can't believe I caught on fire. That was so badass!"

Sabine starts unbuttoning her top. I tell her my stop-at-third-base rules, that I can do Almost Everything, but Not Quite Everything. She nods and keeps unbuttoning. "You took charge when I was in trouble. You hit me really hard."

"I feel awful about that. I've never hit a girl in my life."

"I'm saying I *liked it*, David. And if it happens again, I'll like it again."

I have no idea what to do with that comment. I wanted her to like my fucked-up, manly karate knuckles, but she is taking things up a notch. I look at her breasts, which are naked now to the air. She slithers off her black pants too, then taps her foot against her huge shoulder bag which is on the floor. "Guess what I brought?"

I panic, picturing leather masks and nipple clamps, possibly given to her by members of Megadeth. "I don't know."

She steps out of her panties. "It's something you'll like."

Stripped now, she pulls from her bag her pink concierge vest and skirt. She shows them to me with her eyebrows raised. She is tall and skinny, with a jet-black pubic thatch.

"I'm not coy, like some girls." She puts on her concierge outfit and arranges her breasts beneath the vest. "I'm confident and kinky."

"Sure," I say. "Yes. Me, too."

I'm standing and she kneels in front of me. "I think you know what I'm about to do down here. Or should I be coy and *not* do it? If you want it, you should demand it, with no regard for my feelings."

She seems to hate softness, romance, even civility.

"Um, please do it," I say.

"That wasn't very demanding."

"Please, *please* do it?"

She sighs. I am not demanding enough. But she does it anyway. As she does she takes my hands and guides them to her hair. I stroke her hair and she makes a displeased sound. I grab her hair roughly. Yes. This is what she wants. I yank her head just slightly toward me and she makes a thrilled sound. When I yank harder, she gives me a thumbs-up and picks up her pace.

Sabine begins staying over on Fridays, which are her nights off. She always comes to my place, saying I can't crash at her aunt and uncle's in Queens. She usually hangs out till Saturday evening, then goes to work at the hotel. When she clears out each Saturday, I call my Georgetown friend Daphne Lowell.

Daphne is living in her hometown of Tapwood, Vermont. She teaches English at Tapwood Academy, the boarding school where her father is headmaster, and she proctors in a girls' dorm. Daphne is whip-smart and a great writer. I mail her my stories and she mails me her poems.

One night on the phone she says, "You're too good of a person."

I'm sitting on my bedroom window ledge. I look at the grimy brick courtyard outside when I talk to Daphne, because her voice elevates all the junk in the courtyard, all the scuzzy cats and limp laundry on clotheslines.

"What do you mean?"

"You're too morally good in your stories. They're G-rated. Your writing needs more danger . . . more mess."

I think sometimes about hopping a train north and busting into Daphne's bedroom at midnight and proposing. I wonder if that would be dangerous enough for her.

"David, stop writing bullshit. You're not an *Anne of Green Gables* guy. Write the raw truth."

OVER THE WINTER my father frequently crashes on my couch. He has started a company that sells automotive fleet maintenance software, and he has potential clients in the city. He drives down from Rochester to schmooze them, then he and I cook burgers at my place and cheer for the

Knicks on TV. One morning I take him to Mass at Corpus Christi Church next door to my apartment.

I love this church. My Irish great-grandmother, my mother's Nana, worked as a cook here in the 1920s. Plus it's where the mystical monk and writer Thomas Merton was baptized. There are no night Masses, but the Sunday High Mass is solemn and beautiful. Most everything but the readings and sermon is in Latin, and there's Gregorian chant and incense and nothing nifty. It's a long Mass, which to my surprise makes my father impatient. Afterward he and I walk in Riverside Park.

"All that Latin bugs me," my father says. "I had enough of that as a kid."

We sit on a park bench and look at wan winter sunlight on the Hudson.

"Plus the prison inmates I'm dealing with in my outreach program would have no use for that service. It wouldn't be the truth to those guys."

I nod. My father is advancing toward becoming a Catholic deacon and he keeps me up to date on his homiletics classes. Always a hands-on guy, he is struggling with the idea of having to serve liturgically upon ordination. He's willing to, but mostly he wants to lead out in the world. At his new company he wants to hire ex-cons and train them as computer programmers.

"I don't love the Latin either," I tell him, "but sometimes the bells and incense help me find the Bottom." It just slips out.

"The Bottom?" My father gives me a skeptical look.

"Never mind."

"David, I've got another idea for your novel."

I am now writing and workshopping a novel. It starts on Cape Cod and it involves a confused young man who runs away from his family and hits the road. So far I've shown my father only the upbeat opening chapters on Cape Cod before the narrator flees. My father—who loves Cape Cod and used to take our family on vacations there—has been pitching me plotlines. Since he is partially bankrolling my degree, I try sometimes to use his ideas.

"There could be a real-estate scandal," he says now. "You know how I said the one character should be a Hyannis real-estate mogul? Someone could sabotage his properties. The saboteur hides mercaptan canisters in the air ducts of rental homes and the mercaptan drives away renters and ruins the mogul's business."

"What's mercaptan?"

"The stuff that smells like rotten eggs that gets added to natural gas. Come on, David, you knew that."

I did not know that. No one would know that. But my father has wild and baffling engineering knowledge. And I don't want to disappoint him.

"Okay, Dad. Maybe I'll work in the mercaptan."

"Hey, how's Melvin?" he asks.

"Melvin is Melvin."

I am still tutoring Melvin at the Learning Center. Since

our first meeting Melvin and I have struck up a flimsy truce: I try to improve his writing and he tries not to hide in the ficus plants. But his hygiene gets worse with each passing month. He wears the same coffee-stained flamingo sweatshirt to every session and he smells like a gutter. The fact that he never speaks to others makes me think that he is friendless and lonely. So, despite his stench and manic manner, I try to help him. I try to build up the greater assembly.

In February Melvin comes to me with what he says is his most important English paper of the year. The topic is "Seminal Moments in Narrative" and each student has been assigned a novel to use as a source. Melvin has been assigned *The Adventures of Huckleberry Finn.* He sits across from me at our table watching me read his essay.

"It's my best essay yet, right? It focuses on a violent act, which you told me is a smart thing to focus on . . . right?"

Melvin's Huck Finn essay begins:

HUCK FINN THE BOOK HAS SEMINAL MOMINTS, LIKE WHEN HUCK FINN. THE CHARACTER. RIPS UP THE LETTER TO MIS WATSON THAT WOULD CRIMINATE JIM. THE NEGRO SLAVE, HIS FRIEND. HUCK SAYS "THEN I'LL GO TO HELL!" AND RIPS UP LETTER AND IT'S SEMINAL, WHICH MEANS HUCK IS EXCITED. HE IS ENGORGED AND HIS JUICES ARE FLOWING.

I stop reading. "Melvin, you can't submit this to your teacher. Huck Finn is never engorged. His juices are never flowing."

"Sure they are. They must be! This is a seminal scene, this letter-ripping business. My teacher said it was seminal."

"It's seminal because it's a turning point. When Huck tears up the letter, he's choosing loyalty to Jim and to what he believes in. But it's not a sex scene."

Melvin's face is livid. "I worked hard on this. And a scene can't be seminal without being sexual. *Seminal* is from *semen*. Give me my paper."

He takes hold of his essay, which I hold on to for a second longer.

"I don't want you to fail, Melvin."

He wrenches the paper away and hustles out.

ON NIGHTS WHEN I don't have karate class, I practice it at the apartment. After moving the furniture aside in the living room, I spend hours punching and kicking. I have upended a spare bed mattress and placed it against the wall as an opponent. My favorite kick is the spinning back roundhouse. I do it best when I stand on my left leg, wheel around, and strike the mattress with my right heel.

Executing this kick thrills me. I practice it nonstop, somehow needing to. I get good enough that I tear big holes in the mattress. I start carrying the kick in me everywhere, the will of it. Karate is matching something in my spirit. Something fraught is bubbling up in me, gathering to a boil, though I don't know what it is. When I work on my novel, I try to write my way into this fraught place. Or to draw from it.

WEEKS LATER, on a rare Monday night when she is staying over, Sabine sits on my bedroom floor with me. We're playing Scrabble and listening to her Black Flag mix tape, but we keep the volume low because on the other side of my closed door the Mormons are gathered. Sad Dog is doing a slide show for the others, recounting his two-year Mormon mission in South Korea.

I spell a seven-letter word and get lots of points. Sabine swats the board like she's pissed off and tiles go flying. Laughing, she shoves me on my back, lies on top of me and kisses me. Kissing turns to groping. We undress. Henry Rollins is singing "Can't Decide."

Kissing her, I try to guide her onto the bed, but she pulls me to the floor. I kiss her belly, then head south to her lap.

"The most satisfying thing," says Sad Dog out in the living room, "was calling on folks, giving door-to-door witness. The woman you see on this slide invited us in for tea."

Sabine stirs her hips. "Don't stop." She moans loudly. Then she grabs my T-shirt off the floor and shoves it in her mouth. She has never done this before.

"Doan dop," she urges me through her gag.

I peek up from her lap, worried that she isn't getting air. Is this the raw truth that Daphne mentioned?

"Keeb goan!"

"This slide," says Sad Dog, "shows us in Seoul with some pals from Provo."

"Dayffd, reej ubbn joag me."

"Reach up and *choke* you? I'm not going to choke you."

"Fuggin do ib!"

I'm still in her lap, but I reach a hand up and comply tentatively.

"Ommuguh, so fuggin seggsy. Do ib harber."

"This slide," says Sad Dog, "shows a weird vegetable they like over there."

"Harber, Dayffd. Joag me alldaway. Kiw me." *Choke me all the way. Kill me.*

I get my face above Sabine's. The white cotton of my T-shirt swells out of her mouth.

"Um . . . you don't literally want . . . this is just dirty talk, right? Is this dirty talk?"

"Nod derby tok. Weewy do ib." *Not dirty talk. Really do it.*

She shoves her hand between her thighs. "Pwee joag me alldaway. *Kiw me.*"

I shake my head. The want in her eyes is lethal. I keep shaking my head no, and she keeps begging, desperate to blast past herself, to somewhere beyond.

David Schickler

ONE APRIL NIGHT, karate class goes late. My father is waiting at the apartment and we have plans to go out. He just made a big software sale and it's time to celebrate.

As soon as class gets out I hurry home and enter my apartment, still wearing my *gi*. "Dad? You here? Let me grab a quick shower, then we'll get dinner."

"David. Come in here. Now."

His tone means trouble. I find him in the living room. He's sitting on the couch and on his lap is my novel manuscript. The last time we were together I gave him the whole thing to read, and I've been hoping that he'll like it.

His eyes are set on mine, dead serious. "David . . . what in the hell is this?"

"It's my book. My novel."

"How could you have written what's in here? How could you?"

I stare at the floor. I have woven into the novel the plotlines my father suggested, about real estate and mercaptan. But my workshop mates and teacher hated those parts. *Feels forced*, they jotted in the margins. Or *Not pulling its weight* or *This part sucks!*

On the other hand my chapters about the narrator—the mogul's son who runs away from home—have caused buzz. When it comes to the scene where the narrator and the skinhead girl 69 on the floor of a grimy ska bar, everyone says I nailed it.

"I can't believe this." My father sets the manuscript on the floor. "How will we ever show this to your mother or anyone we know?"

"*We* won't do anything, Dad, because it's *my* book."

He widens his eyes, which alone is about enough to stop my heart. "Is that right."

"Um . . . my classmates think that what I'm doing in this novel is . . . gutsy. One of them said that it was strange, but also strangely beautiful."

"I'm not your classmates, I'm your father. And Schickler men don't—"

"Well, I'm not 'Schickler men'! I'm—" I pick up my manuscript and clutch it against my stomach. "I'm just trying to be an artist, Dad. This is just art."

"*The Old Man and the Sea* is art." He stands and points at my pages. "That is pornography. Or rock and roll mixed with pornography, or I don't know what."

"Dad . . . what about those guys in your prison outreach? You say they talk about having hurt people. You say that that's the truth to them. Well, this is like that. Not all stories are temperate or chaste."

"Maybe. But you can't write what you're holding and still become a priest."

"Yes I can! Andrew Greeley . . . he's a priest and an author."

149

"David, he was a priest for a quarter century before he wrote. You think he'd have gotten ordained if he'd come in saying he planned to write bodice rippers?"

I'm stymied. I wish he'd hug me or hit me, anything but judge me.

"You think women will read your perverted stuff and let you baptize their babies?"

"My writing's not perverted! It's . . ."

He is already storming out, off to what will be a solo dinner.

"It's *real*," I say. But I'm talking to myself.

A MONTH BEFORE spring semester ends I'm walking on campus when Melvin runs up to me. He's in his flamingo sweatshirt with the coffee stains. "I've been looking for you at the Learning Center."

"They shifted my hours and I'm there on different days now."

"You were right about my Huck Finn paper. My professor wouldn't accept it and now I might fail."

I'd been eating a bagel as I walked, but now I stash it in my coat pocket. There's a revolting scent coming from Melvin. He smells literally like a latrine.

He pulls out a rolled wad of cash, holds it toward me. "Two hundred dollars. Take it and write my paper for me. Come on, we'll sit here and you can riff about Huck and I'll write it all down. It'll work and I'll pass."

I stare at the money. I'm broke and I could use it.

"That's unethical, Melvin." I inhale only through my mouth. His stench is enough to make me vomit. "And I'm sorry to say this, but you also . . . really smell."

He shrugs. "Yeah, sometimes I don't wear it. It's a pain."

"Sometimes you don't wear what?"

"My colostomy bag. It's not fair that I have to have it on all the time, so sometimes I just go without."

I look at him in shock. The stains on his sweatshirt make a new, awful sense. He is still holding the money toward me and his expression seems impatient, as if to say, *Come on, you wanted mess and raw truth, here they are.*

"You need help, Melvin," I say.

He scowls and jabs my chest with the money wad. "What, you're better than me?"

I bat his arm aside. I've had enough of him, of my father, of the fourteen Books of Mormon in my underwear drawer.

"If you poke me again," I say, "we might have a problem."

His face crumbles and saddens, like he'll cry. Pocketing his cash, he runs off, and I feel sick, sick, sick to my stomach.

"Melvin, wait," I call, too late. He rounds a corner and is gone.

It is my last interaction with him and it haunts me. As a tutor I've failed him, and I've failed my father with my fiction. To combat these failings I practice Shotokan obsessively, especially my spinning back roundhouses. Karate classes end, but I work out alone at my apartment. I get better and better, and my workouts get longer. When I finish I stand under a hot shower with aching muscles. I tell myself that they're good aches, the cost of strength, the growing pains of a fighting soon-to-be monk.

In July I fly to San Francisco. Mason is living there and he has gathered our old Georgetown crew for a weekend. Graham and the Alabama Boys come, plus some girls, including Daphne Lowell. One sunny day we walk on the Embarcadero toward Fisherman's Wharf. Mason points out attractions. I have trouble keeping up due to a weird sensation building in my right calf. I want to be walking next to Daphne, so that she'll sense that my karate-tuned body is as dangerous as my fiction is becoming. Eventually she hangs back as I grimace and soldier forward.

"Are you okay? You're hobbling."

"I'm fine."

She bumps my shoulder with hers. "Can we talk about the concierge?"

"Okay . . ."

The feeling in my calf is intensifying. It smarts but it also feels like a falling away of strength, as if the flesh around my shinbone is losing substance with each step I take. I feel like my leg might buckle and give way.

"David, you and I have some deep talks and . . . well, you never even mention her." Wind is blowing Daphne's hair around her face. "Please don't be upset that I'm saying this, but I feel like you're just clocking time with this girl. I feel like you're cut out for . . . something bolder. More lasting."

Like priesthood, I think. *Or you.*

She says, "There's something else. I'm getting engaged."

I stop short. The pain in my calf is now so bad that I can't keep moving.

"He teaches at Tapwood with me. He's twelve years older, but . . . well, we're in love and we're getting married."

There's a flagpole beside us with a thick concrete base. I sit down on this base. "That's so great," I say, wincing. "You'll be so happy."

"David, are you all right?"

"Um, could you ask Mason how I can get a cab to his place? My leg's out of it."

"What'd you do to yourself?"

"I don't know." I rub my calf.

She frowns at my leg. "Okay. Hold tight." She hurries off.

I massage my calf harder. I remember limping through Berlin with a bum ankle. And I remember the dread, the awful feeling of groundlessness that was there beneath the pain. That dread surges in me now and it says, *At last I've got you.*

Chapter Seven

"TELL ME WHERE IT HURTS," Dr. Greer says.

It is September of my second Columbia year and I'm in Dr. Greer's office at Mount Sinai hospital, downtown. Dr. Greer is in his fifties and completely bald. When he speaks he leans back and looks down at me through thick glasses. He is sitting behind his desk, where he's been since I entered his office, not having stood to shake my hand. He's the specialist the Columbia health center referred me to for my persistent leg pain.

"It hurts all through my right calf," I say. "It's been happening for months. When I walk to school I'm all right for a block and then it starts feeling like someone has my calf in a vise grip and is squeezing it harder and harder. So it feels tight but . . . hollow. Like it's without strength, like it might give way."

"You've pulled a muscle," says Dr. Greer.

"I run a lot and I know what pulled muscles feel like. This is different. My calf feels cramped but empty inside."

"Sciatica," he says. "Nerve-related, referred pain from the spine. We'll run tests. My office will set it up. I have to head to a lecture. Be well, David."

So over the next couple of months tests get run: X-rays and MRIs of my spine and right leg. According to the tests, I'm fine. I have no slipped disks or bone spurs or torn muscles. Yet my right calf is shrinking, atrophying, and the clenching feeling gets worse each day. The five-block walk from my apartment to Dodge Hall on campus takes twice as long as usual. My karate ends.

Soon the problem isn't just in my calf. Spasms of pain flare up deep in my right hip and buttock. Sometimes they're so intense that I grab a wall or a stranger's shoulder so that I won't fall. During some flare-ups my eyes ram shut and I see white and blue fireworks.

"Maybe you have HIV," Dr. Greer tells me in his office one January day.

I throw up a little in the back of my throat. "What?"

"Sometimes a pins-and-needles sensation can occur in the limbs or extremities in the early stages of HIV. Do you think you might have contracted it?"

I stare at him, terrified.

"We'll run a blood test. The results take two weeks to come back, and then we'll discuss those results. Be well, David."

Be well? I think, walking out of his building. *Be well,*

motherfucker? "Be well" is something Ward Cleaver might say to June. It's not what you tell a guy getting tested for HIV.

I take the blood test and in the two weeks that follow I can't write or sleep. I take walks in Riverside Park, enduring hip spasms and clenching in my calf and a nervousness that I now feel all through me. It isn't only fear of HIV. It's that deeper dread, that groundlessness I've felt on and off since Tübingen, and I can't understand it.

One day as I limp beside the Hudson, this dread surges so hard that I stop walking. I lean against a tree and stare at the river, trying to catch my breath. The dread is like a dark, molten thing in my chest, rising up my windpipe, blocking air.

I try to stare at the dread, to scour it, to know it. *You're smart*, I tell myself. *Face it. Figure it out.*

The Hudson's waters are grayish black and rough. Wind kicks at them, making them slap and bicker, and looking at the waves, I suddenly do figure out my dread, at least part of it. I trip over a memory, one I buried long ago but that comes back now. I can smell this memory in my sinuses. It oozes between my fingers . . .

. . . I'M YOUNG, and the dark path in the Black Creek woods is my main haunt, but the rest of the golf course attracts us kids, too. In the summers we climb trees in the woods, and the vines around the trees grow so thick that one day when I stumble and fall headfirst off a high branch, I get caught in a web of vines and never hit the ground. And the rest of the golf course seems like that, like something made to catch me, delight me. The landscaping of the eleventh hole is beautiful: five hundred yards of fairway with the creek along one edge and a large blue pond and mammoth shrubs near the green.

I love the dark path best, but the whole golf course is a buffer between me and life's troubles. In these woods and on these fairways there is no litter, no squawking TV, no bullies giving me wedgies, nothing that doesn't feel natural and good. That's why it's a disturbance when Tommy fucks Lesley on my path.

But then comes another disturbance, just a month after Tommy screws Lesley. It is July and the greenskeepers drain the eleventh-hole pond. They're scheduled to widen or dredge it, but all summer long they never do. Instead the great brown pock that was the pond's bottom lies exposed. Hundreds of long-lost golf balls dot the surface of this pock and the greenskeepers never skim them away. My friends and I often scavenge in the woods for lost balls which we clean and sell to golfers, so the drained pond looks like a jackpot.

One afternoon I'm at the pock's edge with two of the Langini brothers. Mike Langini, who's thirteen like I am, strips to his briefs.

"Schickler, you watch for golfers. Danny, hand the net out to me when I say."

Danny is Mike's kid brother. The Langinis are fearless hooligans.

"Let's make some fucking money," says Mike.

He steps onto the drained bottom of the pond and sinks up to his chest. The mud makes a furious sucking sound and releases a wafting stench of sulfur.

"Mike!" I shout. "Get out of there!"

"Minghia," Mike says.

Then, like nothing serious is occurring, he grins and reaches for golf balls that are within arm's length. He tosses them onto shore, but he's already sinking farther, up to his armpits, disappearing from view.

"Fuck." Mike sounds annoyed. "Better reach me out the net, Danny."

Danny does, but he's short so I help him shove the long bamboo pole toward Mike. We can barely jut it far enough, but Mike finally grabs it. We pull. I feel through the pole handle a power working against us, trying to claim Mike's body. This mud, it's alive and willful. It wants my friend.

"Mike," I beg. "Mike!"

Sucks and slurps of sound come from the mud around Mike's chest. They are awful, hungry noises. We reel Mike closer, but he's still sinking down, almost up to his neck, and I can't reach him with my hands yet.

Help us, Lord! I pray. *HELP!*

I pull on the pole with all my strength. Mike churns through the mud another couple inches, then Danny and I finally get him by a shoulder. As we pull him out, the mud gives a last, spiteful, violent suck. Then Mike is on land.

"Mike." I hug him hard.

"Schickler, you faggot, let go." Mike snorts, shaking his head, looking out at the hundreds of balls. "What a fucking crock. We'll never get them."

That night I wrap my sheets and blankets around myself and curl in a ball on the floor of my basement bedroom. I need solidity. Even my mattress is too soft, too much like mud. The Langinis are insane with bravado, but I know the truth: Mike almost drowned. If he'd stepped out even a foot farther, he would've been beyond our reach and we would've watched the mud close over him and take him away from us, from his mother, his future. There'd been no adults around who could've rescued him.

I lie on my floor, trembling. That mud is not far away. It's waiting, ready to pull down anyone who steps in it. The power it had as it sucked at Mike overwhelms me.

I've always trusted nature. I've felt that the dark path, the creek, the woods have cared about me because they're part of the world and God made the world and God cares about me and Mike and all people. But that pond mud is part of the world and that mud didn't care about Mike today. It would've swallowed him or me as easily as it would've a rock. And worse, it had *wanted* to swallow Mike. It had been in its nature to try to take him under.

I squeeze my eyes shut. *No,* I think, *God loves me. He loves me, He protects me, He cares what happens to me.*

But then I think of the temptation of those golf balls on

that mud. Part of me says sure, mud is dangerous, like sharks and lightning. But those shiny balls lying on that mud like bait . . . that detail seems designed, arranged by some cruel force.

The Langinis and I aren't the only kids who find and sell golf balls. Tons of local kids do. And there's a public playground near that mud, on the other side of a thin strip of trees. And some kids who play there unattended are barely five and sometimes they wander onto the golf course.

As I lie on my floor, my blood races. The pond mud fills me up inside, drowning out my organs and bones, obliterating safety.

You made a mistake, I tell God. *That mud shouldn't be out there.*

I barely sleep.

The next day I begin a ritual that I keep up all summer, at least on fair-weather days. Every afternoon for an hour before dinnertime, when the playground is busiest, I hide in the shrubs near the drained pond. I bring binoculars and a rope. I keep my binoculars trained on the trees between the playground and golf course. I'm scared just sitting near the mud, but I'm here to correct God's mistake. I will make sure that no child strays near the mud. Or I'll rescue any kid who falls in.

I'm too scared to tell anyone but I start dreaming at night of mud pouring into my mouth and nose and ears. I wake up sweating, my heart pounding. In autumn the greenskeepers fill the pond back in with water and make life look right again, and my nightmares subside. I force myself to forget the mud. I let God's error go . . .

. . . BUT NOW over a decade later as I stand by the Hudson, it's back, the quicksand in my chest. The dread, the scary, ground-less sensation that plagued me in Tübingen and since: it isn't similar to my old quicksand feeling, it *is* that feeling, back again, stronger.

I stare at a Riverside Park tree, at a scampering squirrel. Do-ing this—gazing at small pieces of nature—usually clears my mind. Not today.

I close my eyes. *Lord, all I need to feel better is a negative HIV test, right? Once that comes, this dread will vanish, right? I'm trying to bear my hip pain without self-pity. But can You just speak once and tell me that this dread will pass?*

I hear nothing.

Two weeks later, the test comes back negative. I don't have HIV. But my right calf is still atrophying. Compared to my left, it is barely half the size around, and the spasms in my hip are constant and acute. When a spasm comes, someone may as well be thrusting a sword in my ass, skewering the place where my femur meets my hip socket.

"I really think you're all right," says Dr. Greer casually, in February. "Your sciatic might be a tad inflamed." He yawns.

"Just try a little ibuprofen to relax it. Two with breakfast, two with lunch, and two with dinner. Be well, David."

As I limp home, I write a short play in my head:

Dr. Greer is in a dungeon, locked in an iron maiden, dying. The Dungeon Master sits nearby, yawning, flipping through a magazine.

DR. GREER: Aaaaaaaaaaaarrrrrrrrgh!

DUNGEON MASTER: Your innards might be a tad inflamed from the spikes.

DR. GREER: Fuuuuuuuuuuuucckkk!

DUNGEON MASTER: I have to go give a lecture. Be well, Dr. Greer.

In the coming days I trump Dr. Greer's advice and take three ibuprofen pills, three times a day. When that doesn't work, I take five pills with each meal, and then switch from ibuprofen to extra-strength Tylenol, again five pills at a time. It still doesn't help. Every night from midnight until two, I watch *Mystery Science Theater* on TV and drink most of a six-pack of Bass or the whole six-pack. But my pain perseveres and my dread grows. It turns to outright panic.

"You just need something to take your mind off your hip," Sabine says, and she pulls me into bed.

"Just read this," Sad Dog says, and he gives me my twentieth, then twenty-first, then twenty-second Book of Mormon.

"Get some R and R," Graham tells me on the phone. He's calling from San Francisco, where he's a line cook at a restaurant.

"Stop being Catholic," Mason says, calling from L.A., where he's in film school. "Your body is bucking a bullshit belief system."

Nothing any of them says helps. Beer, friends, kisses—it all gets obliterated by my hip pain or dragged under by the quicksand in my chest.

I write nothing. I shuffle around Morningside Heights. When a crosswalk light changes, giving people thirty seconds to cross Broadway, I can barely make it from one sidewalk to the median island.

"Hmm," says Dr. Greer, in April. "I think the pain is psychosomatic."

I roll up my pant legs to my knees. My right calf is a skinny joke beside my healthy left one. I let him see this. "I'm not imagining this, Doctor. Something is *wrong* in me. Something is tweaked or fucked-up inside me."

"Maybe you need a second opinion. Be well, David."

I leave his office. Teary-eyed, I call my mother. "I have to come home."

"You can come home whenever you need to," she says. "Tonight, if you need to. But try to offer what you're going through up to the Lord."

So I stay in New York for two more weeks, limping through my final classes, offering my pain to the Lord. But when the spasms come, offering dies fast. It becomes begging. *Please, make it stop. Please, Lord, please.*

I MOVE HOME to Rochester in June and live in my old basement bedroom. I see our family doctor, then a neural specialist. Neither can figure out my problem and in desperation I make an appointment with a chiropractor, Matt Argento, my old neighbor from Twin Circle Drive. Matt's high school football stardom earned him his way to college, he now has a beautiful wife and a cool car, and the colossal physique he always did.

Everyone around here is proud of Matt. He still looks and talks like a jock, but he's friendly. When I go into his office he shouts, "Minghia! I ain't seen you in years! All right, take off your jeans, get on the table, let's look at you."

I do as directed. I've already told Matt the history of my injury, but as soon as he sees my shriveled lower right calf, his face goes dead serious.

"Oh, man." He puts a palm on my calf. "Oh, minghia. Look at this leg. That motherfucker."

"Who?"

"That doctor in New York. He let *this* condition get *this* far? Minghia, I should drive down and fuck him up."

I'm surprised. "Matt, I did this to myself. I was doing these spinning karate kicks and—"

"Yeah, but when did you stop the karate and start seein' the doc?"

"Ten months ago."

"And the doc took tests and gave you pills, but never friggin' touched you, right?"

I tell him that he's basically right.

Matt works his jaw under the skin. He moves my leg around more, inspects my hip. "David, this is *treatable shit*, okay? However it started, what's happening now is piriformis syndrome. Your piriformis muscle—that's a muscle deep in your ass!—was maybe hurt by karate, but it's now slackened from underuse, okay? And it's impinging on your freakin' sciatic nerve. That can cause atrophy in the calf, okay? But it's treatable." He shakes his head. "And when I see *treatable shit* and a doctor was *supposed* to treat it and *didn't*, I get pissed. Especially when it happens to one of my people . . . okay?"

He sounds like Dirty Harry. I haven't seen him in ten years, but he just called me one of his people the way my other Italian buddies growing up introduced me to strangers as their cousin.

"Unlike that Manhattan pussy, I ain't afraid to touch you. I'm gonna fuckin' whale on your hip, okay? Crack the shit out of it. *Promote* some *blood flow* to your fuckin' piriformis. I'm gonna whale on your hip for a few weeks, then you'll be out of pain. How's that freakin' sound, huh?"

"Good," I say.

So in the coming weeks Matt whales on my hip. He cracks

the shit out of it. And everything he promises comes true. In less than a month my hip and leg pain start to ease up.

But the quicksand in my chest doesn't. All I've thought about for months are the twinges and throbs in my hip and leg, how to kill them. But now that Matt is killing them, I feel a void, and the quicksand is rushing in, filling that void. When I lie on the couch and watch *Cheers* reruns, my heart pounds. When I drive, my hands shake on the wheel. I can't get enough air in my lungs.

Early one August morning I walk out onto the eleventh hole of the golf course. There are no golfers out yet. I stand beside the pond and stare at it. It is silver, like the dawn-gray clouds. I stand where I stood when Danny and I rescued Mike from the mud.

See, you jumpy fuck? I tell myself. *There's a full pond here. There's no quicksand here, or inside you. Calm down and man up.*

But the black suction in my chest won't quit.

So I walk on the path. I go to my spot, stare at the shadows that used to bring me comfort. I even step into the woods and dig in the ground, looking for a piece of broken china, thinking that if I find one like I used to, I'll feel okay, I'll know where I am. I beg the Lord to speak, to break His silence.

Instead the rival darkness, the black panic, tugs at me inside. It's sucking my heart down. It wants me to drown.

Suddenly my hip gives out. The spasms have been coming

less often since I've been working with Matt, but this one is a doozy. I wipe out in the dirt, landing hard on my elbow.

Lying there, I try to think only rational thoughts. I fell down, I think, only because my hip gave out, and that happened because of piriformis syndrome, which was caused by karate and then went untreated . . .

But the dread in me says, *This time, I wiped you out, David. I knocked you on your ass. Because I'm sick of waiting. Have I got your attention?*

I wait. And then the dread speaks. *David, I've waited so long to tell you this . . .*

I somehow know what's coming next.

. . . You'll never be a priest.

I sit there in the dirt. Dew seeps through my jeans.

Never, David.

Back home my father is getting ready to paint our front door because my sister Anne Marie is getting married in a few weeks and out-of-town guests will stay at our house, and my father wants the place looking sharp. He is waiting for me to help him.

But I can't even stand up. Because somehow, right this instant, adult life has arrived. And I've always believed deep down that everything I've ever done—running, writing, Georgetown, Columbia, karate, romance, pain, all of it—it has all been apprenticeship, steps on my path to priesthood. I've been preparing myself for God, for a simple, solitary life where I'll worship

His Truth, where I'll empty myself out and let His dark, weight-less, mystical grace fill me and claim me for the Jesuits.

No, says the panic now. *Not you.*

And the panic is right. I know it. I finally feel it. It will never happen. That life, contemplative life and priesthood . . . it won't have me. Without saying why, it is vacating my heart, breaking up with me, suddenly, now, forever. It was the most basic thing I believed, the ground I stood on, even when I wasn't thinking about it. And it's gone.

My stomach seizes up.

"DAD?"

"David, where have you been? Grab that tarp and let's cover your mom's flowers here to keep the paint off them."

He's standing up on the front porch and I'm on the lawn below. I hand him the tarp and he spreads it over the flowers. I've just limped back from the path.

"Dad."

He hears my tone and turns. "What is it?"

I look at him, my thoughts zipping and tumbling.

Dad, you're so . . . decent. Look at all that you do. You take care of your kids, you give to charities, you counsel prisoners, you never get drunk, you read Catholic Digest, *you take Mom to Anne Murray concerts, you pray with her in bed each night, I've heard you two whispering—*

"David." He steps off the porch. "Tell me what's wrong."

—and what do I do, Dad? I get plastered and I give head to a nymphomaniac concierge and I tell myself that it's semi-chaste because at least it will never get her pregnant. And I hate Anne Murray. I freaking hate her. And I love wine and blow jobs and the feel of the word "fuck" in my mouth and I have to have these things and—

"I can't do it, Dad."

"How's that?"

I sit on the porch. I can smell something like metal, or rotten eggs, in my sinuses. "Oh fuck, Dad. I can't be a priest."

I sob. He sits beside me. He looks alarmed and hugs me.

"David, my God, it's all right."

"It's not, it's not."

He holds me.

"Dad, I don't even know if I still . . ."

"Just tell me."

My breath keeps bucking. The quicksand, the sucking panic, is pulling under everything I've ever loved or used to define myself. *The Great Gatsby* and "Rosalita" are going under, and so are my writing, my running. God Himself. Scripture says that I should love the Lord with all my heart, soul, strength, and mind. But even though I've always tried to do that, God is going under anyway. He is drowning and disappearing, and I can't save Him.

I look at my father, stunned. "I don't even know if I still . . . believe."

My father doesn't say anything. He just holds me.

I KEEP UP my sessions with Matt, and he tells me to lift weights so that I'll wean myself off his adjustments and strengthen my piriformis. But each day, as my hip and leg get stronger, my panic grows. For months my calf was disappearing . . . now hope is. I feel twitchy and sick. I remember what Merton wrote, that despair is self-absorption, but I can't get out of the quicksand. The mere thought of Mass makes me nauseous.

I think, *I'll never be a priest, and God might be a lie. I'll never be a priest, and God might be a lie.*

I call Sabine in New York. I tell her that I always thought that I'd become a Jesuit, but that I can't. She gets pissed off.

"Your church did this to you. All that celibacy crap. They screwed you up."

I stay silent.

"Fly back down to see me before the wedding. My aunt and uncle are away and you can stay with me in Queens. I'll make you feel better, I promise."

"Okay," I say.

We hang up. Late that night I can't sleep, so I get up and go outside. I wander out on the golf course. It's September, dark and chilly.

I think, *Your sister's getting married, your hip is healing, be happy. Do* not *panic. Just* resolve *not to.*

Resolved, I walk on. I hum a song. The woods are placid. I break into sobs.

The next morning I go to see a therapist, a psychologist friend of my parents. I tell him that I'll never be a priest, that God might be a lie, that I know there are greater problems in the world, but that I don't know what to do, what I am.

The therapist says, "You have a big ball of stress inside you. We have to crack it open, get to its nucleus."

I say that I feel pretty cracked open already.

When I get home, I sit on the living room floor. No one else is home.

See? You're not panicking right now. You visited a therapist, and now you're all better. See?

The phone rings and I answer. I try to sound healthy. "Hello?"

"David, it's Daphne Lowell."

I picture her beautiful, married face. I haven't spoken to her in months.

"Hey," I say shakily.

"Your Manhattan number is disconnected. How are you?"

I tell her. It takes an hour.

Daphne says, "You need to come up here. To Vermont, to talk to my father."

"Why?"

"I was originally calling because we need a new English teacher, and I told my dad to interview you. But given what you just said, you *have* to come for the interview. Come, like, tomorrow."

"Why?"

"Just come."

"I can't. My sister's getting married Saturday and before that I'm supposed to go see Sabine."

"Forget the concierge. And you'll get back in time for your sister. You need this."

I turn my brain off. "Okay."

The next day, on the flight to Burlington, I have my worst attack yet. Buckled in a seat beside a stranger, I clench my fists and feel sweat down my spine.

I'll never be a priest, and God might be a lie.

The quicksand sucks air from my lungs. It might suck this plane down, crash it.

You're a fucking baby, I think. But I'm still gripping the seat dividers like mad.

A flight steward looks at me, concerned. "Afraid of flying?"

I'm not, but I nod.

I put on my headphones, turn on my Walkman, play a mix tape. It's U2, then Creedence, then the Billy Bragg song "Greetings to the New Brunette."

I listen to this ballad, one of the rawest and sweetest I've ever heard.

The plane is steady, no turbulence, but inside I flail, try to grab hold of some memory, or future. And then she's there in me, strong and unsinkable.

I say out loud what I still love and want to cling to.

"Mara," I say.

Chapter Eight

"WHY SHOULD I HIRE you to teach English?" asks Clement Lowell.

Clement is Daphne's father. We're sitting in his headmaster's office at Tapwood Academy, in the small mountain town of Tapwood, Vermont. The town is high up in the state, in the Northeast Kingdom. It's late September and on the winding back-road drive to Tapwood from Burlington (Daphne picked me up at the airport), I stared out the window at foliage the bright orange color of hazmat suits. The view didn't calm me. And here in this oaken office, I'm tweaking out, shredding my cuticles with my thumbnails. I want to bolt, but to where? It's eight at night, an odd time for an interview, but Clement said he wanted to be sure we'd be alone.

He is tall and thin and has a no-nonsense bearing, like a

founding father. I can picture him signing the Constitution. Earlier at his home I had roast beef with him and his wife, Beatrice, and Daphne. The Lowells are putting me up in their guest room.

"You shouldn't hire me," I say.

Clement is behind his desk. There's a picture on the wall of a river, a fisherman.

"Why not?"

"I think maybe I'm going crazy."

"Why?"

Daphne has told me that he's a deacon at the Catholic church down the road. I dump my story to Clement. I say that I'll never be a priest, that God might be a lie, that Catholicism has been my home all my life and now home just isn't there. I tell him about my horny fiction, my sexy concierge girlfriend. I tell him that I drink and curse, that my heart is a swamp, that Mara Kincannon is the only thing in it that's not sinking.

"And I keep doing this . . ." I wipe my cheeks. "I keep bursting into tears. My hands keep shaking. I may check into a psych ward a week from now."

"Teach here for a week first."

I don't know how to respond to that.

"David, you're not crazy, you're humiliated." He looks out the window. "When I was your age, I was in the seminary. I was their ace candidate for priesthood and I got handpicked to get sent to study in Rome. A great honor. A week before they sent me, I quit. In those days, if you left, you left in disgrace, in the middle of the night, with your tail between your legs. That's how I did it."

"Why'd you quit?"

"I couldn't live without a woman. I loved the sacraments, the Eucharist. But . . ." He trails off. "A life with a woman, with sex . . . I couldn't do without it. So I bailed. But I felt like a selfish prick."

I'm locked in on his words.

"Afterward it was pretty awful. But I had to go through it."

"Why?"

He shrugs. "Maybe so I could be here, telling you you're not nuts."

Black pressure squeezes my lungs. My pulse shoots. *Fuck, not again—*

"Breathe," Clement says. "Ride it out."

I clench and unclench my fists. "My faith is . . . gone."

"Then stop thinking about it. Just do two things. For one, move up here in a couple weeks and start teaching."

"I've tutored, but I've never taught. I'll suck."

"Then that'll be on me."

"What's the second thing?"

"You already know. And if you really want to avoid going crazy, do it now. You'll always regret it if you don't."

I meet his gaze. "I don't know where she is."

"Find out."

———

LATER THAT NIGHT, from the Lowells' house, I call Graham and Mason and other Georgetown friends. One finally has the information I need: Mara is in Boston. The friend gives me a work phone number.

In the morning, Daphne brings me to the Burlington airport. I'm supposed to fly to New York to see Sabine for a night and then continue on to Rochester. I tell the ticket agent to change my itinerary and fly me to Boston rather than JFK. Hours later I land at Logan. I find a pay phone and call Sabine. I feel terrible lying, but I say that I'm stuck in Vermont, that the interviews will go another day, that I'll call again soon. She sounds suspicious. When we hang up, I try to make the call I've come here to make, but I'm too nervous.

I think, *I need to be as close to Mara as possible.*

I take a cab to Quincy Market.

I find a pay phone beside Faneuil Hall, figuring that it is the city's nexus, so she must be close. I put in money and dial and it rings five times.

"Hello?"

From old instinct, I say, "It's me."

There's a pause.

"Hey," Mara says softly.

It's been two and a half years since we've seen each other or talked. We ask about each other's families while I feed coins into the phone and lacerate my cuticles. Mara tells me what her job is. I immediately forget.

"Are you on a pay phone?"

"Uh, yes. Actually I'm here. In Boston. I was hoping to see you."

She agrees to meet for a drink at six, after work. She suggests Pizzeria Uno in Faneuil Hall. We hang up and I circumnavigate Faneuil Hall about three hundred times in four hours.

At six I enter Uno's. Mara shows up five minutes later. She's in black boots, a long black skirt, and a cream-colored sweater. Her hair and eyes and smile are the same clobbering team as ever. She hugs me.

"I invited Ellen to come too!" she says. "She'll be here any minute."

Ellen is her younger sister, who loved to pal around with me and Mara.

A hostess leads us to a table.

"Are you walking funny?" Mara asks. "Limping?"

"A little."

We sit. I look around at the huge old-timey black-and-white photos of Chicagoans doing blue-collar work in the 1940s.

We order something. My hands shake under the table. I know that she picked this place for its lack of intimacy, just like she invited Ellen as a buffer. To make it a trifecta, Mara says that her boyfriend arrives in town tonight. It's not Akoni, but some other guy. He's an architect! Or something. He travels a lot! Or something.

"He sounds great," I say. I hope he died an hour ago.

I keep looking at the door, waiting for Ellen to come in and station herself between me and the river-rapids scar under Mara's hair. I can't talk, can't tell Mara anything real, not if her kid sister is coming.

We eat and pay the check. Ellen never shows.

"Where are you staying?" Mara asks. "I have to pick my boyfriend up at Logan, but I can drop you."

I'm staying nowhere, but I name a waterfront hotel. She drops me at it, we hug good-bye, and she drives away. I don't have money for a hotel. I walk to the docks and stare at the harbor, thinking back over our conversation.

After I get cold, I pull my address book out of my suitcase. It has lots of scribblings and crossings out, and I paw through it until I find someone who I think still lives in Boston, my friend Neil. We grew up together, and his parents believed in making very strong Manhattans.

I call him and spill my story. He picks me up, takes me to his apartment, serves me very strong Manhattans, and lets me crash.

In the morning I call Mara again and try to be more forthright. "I need to see you today. And please, no Ellen. No boyfriend."

She agrees, but says she can meet only for lunch. She requests Uno's again. I meet her there at noon. We sit at the same table. Most everyone around us is dressed for work, in sleek suits and skirts. Sunlight floods in the windows, and Mara launches into a story about her sister Mavis. It is a nifty story.

"Mara, please . . . stop. Please let me talk."

I can tell that she's afraid to, that she suspects something. She looks down at her lap and nods once, like *okay*, and then looks back up, giving me the green of her eyes. Either the rest of my life is about her doing that or it isn't.

"Mara," I say. "Mar."

It's never been harder for me to turn air into words, but I tell her. I tell her that I'm still in love with her, that I've never stopped being in love with her. I tell her that I'll never be a priest, that God might be a lie. I tell her that I've been rolling around in bed for two years with a girl I don't care deeply for, that I tried to be a fighter and fucked my body up, maybe permanently, and that I can't get enough breath, that I'm dizzy and scared and not right. I tell her that I know that people can't save each other, but that I had to come see her, because . . .

I stop talking. The panic tugs at me. I stare at the parmesan cheese shaker on the table, feeling the stupidness of saying all that I am in this place.

Mara takes my hand across the table.

"I'm so sorry, Mara. I'm sorry that . . . I thought I was going to be a certain kind of man. And I never talked to you about it. And I think that's what came between us."

We're looking into each other's eyes. She looks as scared as I am, but she holds my hand and I feel like we're trying to be something together. Brave, maybe.

I tell her that whatever fuel I've been driving on up till now in life, I've run out of it. All I feel capable of is being here. I say that I'm too exhausted to share words or time with anyone else, to want anyone else. I tell her that this is rude, presumptuous, and melodramatic, but that it's also true. "I just . . . I love you."

She sits quietly, crying a little. She's wearing black pants and a dark gray fisherman's sweater. She looks like what she is, a New England Irish world-beater. Her pizza sits uneaten.

"I've been thinking about you a lot lately too," she says. "A lot. And my sisters keep asking me, 'Do you ever think you'll see Dave again?'"

I wait for her to say more. I think, *David, just because this feels like the fulcrum conversation of your life doesn't mean that it is.* Then Mara squeezes my hand and it is after all.

She says, "I miss you."

"I miss you, too."

"I don't know what to do with this. With your being here, saying all this."

"I know."

"I have a boyfriend."

"I know."

We hold hands. Ice cubes float in her glass of Coke. Why do people have careers and meetings? I only want her. I'm scared shitless.

She says, "I have to think about this."

I FLY HOME to Rochester. Inside me is the good-bye embrace Mara gave me. She also gave me her home phone number and told me to call her from Vermont in a couple weeks.

My sister gets married. During the wedding ceremony, I stand on the altar with the other groomsmen and smile and try not to shred my cuticles.

In the morning I call Sabine and tell her as much of the truth as I can. I say that as near as I can tell, I'm having a nervous breakdown. I tell her that she's great, but that my heart is deeply fucked right now, that I'm lost, that I'm so sorry but that I can't be with her anymore . . . I can barely be with myself.

"You've lied to me this whole time," she says. "You could have trusted me and talked about it, but you kept it in. You lied."

I don't argue.

"Your church did a fucking number on you."

I don't argue with that either. And then we hang up.

―――――――

I MOVE UP to Vermont. I drive there at night and on the way I listen to my Billy Bragg cassette, playing "Greetings to the New Brunette" over and over, maybe thirty times in a row. An attack comes somewhere around Lake George. The quicksand fills my throat. My hands shake so hard on the steering wheel that I yank it too hard in one direction and send the car into a skid. I pull over, park, get out, kneel in the roadside gravel. I'm on a two-lane Adirondack road and there are no other cars, just woods, brisk air, and sky.

I realize that I'm not just sad, I'm livid, too. I stare up at the dark sky.

We were supposed to be something together, I think. *I wanted to end up Yours, only Yours. And now You don't want that, You don't want me, and I feel fucking worthless, do You understand that? And maybe the joke's on me, maybe You're a lie, because I've listened all my life, I've prayed and listened, and You've never said one fucking thing. And never mind me, how about Graham and Mason, arguing with me about You all these years, kicking at Your door, never getting word one from You? And how about every child dying from starvation or from the bites of those huge pink poisonous jungle spiders I saw on TV? What possible purpose could You have had for creating those creepy pink fuckers?*

Seriously, are You off talking to dying kids in distant lands, and that's why I'm not hearing from You now, when I need You?

Are You off speaking comfort into their little ears while their bellies distend and they breathe their fragile last and their mothers wail and put them in the ground?

I close my eyes. *If You're real, if You're there, please . . . give me Mara. Or give Mara and me to each other. If You give that, I'll have a path, a joy. I'll have Something rather than the Nothing that is sucking me down.*

Chapter Nine

FIVE DAYS LATER I am standing in a classroom at Tapwood Academy, wearing a bright yellow mask. Standing beside me is Alex Bergeron, a pudgy, gray-haired man who will spend the next two weeks teaching me how to teach high school English before I'm trusted with my own students.

Alex is wearing a mask too, a black one. Both of our masks are the ornate kind that cover only the eyes, the sort that Shakespeare characters wear to balls. We each hold a xeroxed copy of the Edgar Allan Poe story "The Cask of Amontillado." We are "performing" the story for the ten senior students before us.

It's my first day of teaching. I walked into this room minutes ago and Alex, already in his mask, introduced himself to me—in front of the students—by putting the yellow mask over my eyes as he chuckled. He handed me the story and whispered, "You're Fortunato!"

"I don't understand."

He tapped the story in my hands. I glanced at the title.

"I don't know this story."

"Sure you do," Alex whispered. "Sorry that I don't have the cap and bells, but you look like a jester. All right, let's do this."

Then in a booming voice Alex began reading the story aloud, complete with cackles and aggrieved harrumphs, like a Central Casting madman. He's been pointing to me each time it is my—Fortunato's—turn to speak.

He is pointing at me now.

I look at the next line of text. "'Amontillado,'" I read.

Alex puts his hands on his hips, vamping. "'I have my doubts.'"

"'Amontillado!'" I declare.

Alex rubs his chin demonstratively. "'And I must satisfy them.'"

I say, "'Amontillado.'"

The students are staring at us with a look I know well. It's the same look that my neighbor Mike Langini wore for years while he stared at our nun teachers back in grade school. It is a look that says, *What the fuck is happening? Why are adults such tards?*

I don't know what's happening either. I've only become more disoriented and panicky since arriving in Tapwood. When I got here five nights ago Clement and Daphne helped me move into an off-campus apartment attached to an Academy art teacher's house. Each day since, I've walked around this hilltop town of seven thousand people, trying to get my bearings. There's a grist mill, and postcard foliage on the trees, and one quaint bookstore and one quaint newspaper, but I can't grasp any of it. I'm so scared now that I'm stupid. I keep blanking out. The quicksand is in my brain, pulling under even simple things. Each morning I stare at spoonfuls of Special K, wondering why they're headed toward my face, guided by my hand.

"The next line is yours," a gray-haired man whispers to me.

I look at him. I think his name is Amontillado. I can't breathe.

"Turn the page," the man encourages me. "Hey, stop clenching your fists. Jesus, are you crying?"

"No," I lie. I lift my jester's mask and wipe my eyes.

MY APARTMENT is on Mulligan Street, a mile from the Academy. Daphne lives just four doors down in a house with her husband, Andrew Preevy, and his daughter from a former marriage. Daphne and Andrew both teach English at the Academy. They have me over for dinner one night, after which Daphne walks me home.

"Have you called Mara?"

"It hasn't been two weeks yet."

"Call her tonight."

We walk along. Daphne bumps my shoulder with hers. Her husband is a kind, spooky man who doesn't like me much because he stared into my soul the second I met him and saw how sexy I find his wife.

We reach my apartment. The house it's attached to, the home of art teacher Ed Neville and family, is a clean, well-lighted place. On the lawn in front of my apartment there used to be a tree, but when it got large enough to threaten the house, Ed had most of it cut down. He kept the six-foot-tall stump and had some woodworker carve the stump into a statue of his hero, Knute Rockne.

I look at Knute, stalwart and huge on the lawn, a man famous for being one excellent thing.

Daphne hugs me.

"Go in and call her," she says.

I go in and call Mara. She answers on the third ring.

"About time you called." She laughs her murmuring laugh. I hear a voice in the background that I recognize.

"Ellen's over," says Mara. "I'm helping her with a history paper. What do you know about fossil fuels?"

"We're running out of them," I say. In my head I replay her words, *About time you called. About time you called.*

I try to say funny, attractive things. I tell her about Fortunato and the masks. The phone cord is hangman tight around my fingers.

After a few minutes, Mara sends Ellen into the other room.

"I miss you," she tells me.

I tell her about the Billy Bragg ballad. I tell her that even though she's not a brunette, she's the girl in the song and I'm the guy.

She says, "I'm thinking of you every day. My boyfriend's coming into town again next weekend, and we're supposed to go on a trip, but I don't know . . ."

I wait, knowing that she's thinking, that her eyebrows are pinched together, making a skin ridge of worry between them. When we first dated, if her face screwed up like that, I'd press my thumb to that ridge and bulldoze it for her.

"David, I . . . I have to talk to him. Please . . . I just need some time. I'll be in touch soon, all right?"

We hang up.

In the coming days my hip pain returns. As I limp around the Academy halls, something deep in my right hip socket clicks loudly—and hurts sharply—with about every fifth step I take.

I call Matt Argento and tell him about the clicks, the pain.

"That fuckin' piriformis." He sounds solemn, like he's speaking of an old enemy. "Minghia! It's a tricky muscle, David, the piriformis, and once you fuck it up, it's hard to heal it for good. Also, if you're under stress, that might slow the healing. You dealing with some fuckin' stress?"

I don't feel like going into it, so I make an excuse to get off the phone.

I am now teaching on my own. I've taken over Alex Bergeron's class of ten seniors, and I also teach two sophomore classes. The Academy is unusual since two-thirds of the kids are local day students—many from somewhat poor local families—while the other third are students in the expensive boarding program.

Academy English classes are basic, standard, or accelerated. My sophomores are accelerated, and my seniors are standard.

My seniors don't like me, and, maybe because I'm young, they interrogate me daily. The most vocal ones are Paul and Max, both beefy football jocks; JoBeth, a seventeen-year-old with an infant son at home; and Kira, a bright Swedish girl who feels insulted to be in a standard class.

On my third solo teaching day I sit among them, trying to lead a discussion of *Lord of the Flies*. They were supposed to have read the novel for Mr. Bergeron. I think half of them have opened it.

I ask, "Why does Piggy die, do you think?"

Paul, sitting beside me, nudges my arm. "Hey, Flatlander . . . how come your hip clicks?"

The local kids call me Flatlander. It's a Vermont term for outsiders, for people not from the mountains.

"I know, right?" JoBeth is looking at my hip. Her face is squinched, like she's smelling something off-putting. "I heard it do that, too. It's weird."

"Piggy dies," says Max, "because a rock crushes his head."

I think, *Lucky Piggy.* I think, *I have no business being here, pretending to know more than they do.*

"Yes," I say, "but do you sympathize with him? Does he deserve to die? How do you feel about Roger, the boy who kills Piggy?"

Kira taps her book urgently. "This book is about American exceptionalism."

"Piggy's a pain." Max always sits the farthest from me. He has ever since I wore the Fortunato mask. "They kill him because he's a wuss. Maybe he doesn't deserve it, but that's what happens to wusses."

Kira sighs. "There are no girls in this book."

JoBeth says, "I know, right?"

Out of nowhere my chest fills with panic. I feel all the blood and competence drain from my head.

"Mr. Schickler?" someone says.

"Excuse me." I hobble out into the hall, shutting the door behind me. I rest my cheek against the cool hallway wall, trying to calm my nausea.

I'm holding on to what Mara said. *About time you called*, she said.

MOST NIGHTS I GO to Clement Lowell's house for a couple of hours. One of the few times that the quicksand stops pulling at me is when I sit on one end of Clement's couch while he sits on the other end. He watches TV in silence, in the dark. I close my eyes and just sort of feel Clement watching a show or movie.

Somehow this helps me, maybe because he's at peace with his life. I never fall asleep, I just sit there with my eyes closed and listen to Clement breathing and to the TV dialogue and music, and sometimes I hear the Lowells' dog wander in and out. Clement acts like what I'm doing is normal.

"This film is garbage," he says one night, "but now I'm committed."

I don't open my eyes. "I shouldn't be teaching. I blow. The kids hate me."

"I have to see how this ends," says Clement.

Around ten Clement heads to bed and I leave. I've had insomnia since arriving, but lying in bed or sitting alone in my apartment is unbearable, so each night I drive. I head north through the autumn night on two-lane rural roads while my hip spasms and twinges. I keep the windows open, needing the frigid air. The cold is one of the few things I have in common with Tapwood natives. Because I grew up in upstate New York, I have the cold in me like everyone here does. It's like an instinct in my skin, the cold is, a slapping awake of the senses. It doesn't need to be thought about, only accepted.

One midnight, driving up close to the Canadian border, I find a lake. It is set deep among the surrounding mountains. It has no cottages on its shores, just fir trees on the slopes that wall it in. There's a rock pebble beach on the north shore and I park and hobble out to it and sit. I can see no other cars, buildings, or people. There are clouds blocking the stars and a massive darkness over the black water. I stare at this darkness. If it had substance, I'd kick it, but I can feel nothing in it now, no Person or presence. Thoughts gather and shove in me like prisoners rioting, desperate to break out.

Lord, I think toward the darkness, *You are utter bullshit. Do You know what You are, actually? You're a complete Lack of You. You're a Lack-of-God.*

And don't think that I feel this way just because things suck right now, just because of this awful pain in my leg that's back again. I know life can't be perfect. It wasn't perfect back when Tommy Marzipretta punched me in the stomach at Olympic Roller Rink, and it wasn't perfect when I had mono, and it wasn't perfect when Mara fucked Akoni. But during those times I had You. I had the dark, close sureness of You, and now I have the Lack of You, and it's miserable, okay? And You're a coward for deciding not to exist right when I realize that I can't be a priest, that I can never live for You alone.

I try to calm my thoughts. In the dark silence, I'm shredding my cuticles again. I look at my car. It's a red Chevy Beretta, the first car that I've owned. I bought it right before moving here. I try to be grateful for it, to accept that it's good and mine. I try to do this because talking to Nothing is crazy. But my thoughts won't stop.

Here's what else is bullshit, Lack-of-God. It's bullshit that priests always told me that celibate priesthood is Something Higher. Even Saint Paul said it: he said he wished we could all be like him, "unencumbered," set aside for the work of the Spirit. So, what, that means that the rest of us who aren't called to priesthood, we're called to Something Lower? We're encumbered? Saint Paul said if we aren't strong enough for celibacy, we should marry. He said, "There is no sin in it." Well, whoop-de-fucking-doo. What an exciting reason to be with someone forever, because "there's no sin in it." Is that supposed to make me want to be a married deacon for You? Is that the big selling point, that getting hitched and fucking my wife and loving and honoring her won't send me straight to hell?

Are you getting this, Lack-of-God? Are you getting why my heart and mind and body and soul are exhausted from running through this again and again? If Saint Paul is right, and the solitary, unencumbered path is the most blessed one, then the system is rigged. Either I'm strong and celibate and I devote my life to You as a priest, and I go where the wind of the Spirit pushes me in service of You, and I get the power to turn bread into You, and I live as Saint Paul "wishes" me to . . . or else I'm weak and I succumb to the callings of the flesh and choose married life, but, oh, at least "there's no sin it."

That is a bullshit ultimatum. That's a loaded coin flip where only one side of the coin looks shiny. How can that be the whole story? I've read Your book. I know how Your greatest Priest ever made fishermen's nets strain with their catch, I know how He healed the suffering. I wanted to be part of that power. Why does Your book wax so poetic about the magic of priests and of solitary, miracle-working prophets and leave out so much about the magic of men and women together? Where in Your book is a man like my father, giving out groans while he hugs his wife? Where in

Your book is a girl like Mara, scarred and gorgeous, her eyes filling with secret green fire when she comes? Where in Your book is "Greetings to the New Brunette," a love song from the gutter? Where are those details?

Don't tell me the Song of Songs. That's like twenty pages, that's all the lovers get, a footnote. The rest of Your book, the stuff about priests and prophets doing lonely male work, is thousands of pages.

So is that what I am to You now, Lack-of-God, now that I want Mara back? Am I a footnote, a small thing who can't wield power, a commoner waiting for some bishop's blessing rather than giving to a woman or receiving from her a blessing of my own?

Mara's not a small thing. My love for her isn't small, and it's not Something Lower. So why did You write a book and build a church that are making me feel, tonight, so small and low and second-class compared to priests, to the kind of man I can never be? Are You listening? I've listened for years, now You fucking listen!

"It doesn't matter," I say to the black over the lake. My voice sounds sudden and wrong, like it's against the rules of the dark night air for me to talk.

So I switch back to my inside voice. I pray to the God who isn't there in the shadows anymore.

Please let her love me, I pray. *Let her choose me. Please come back to me just that much.*

Chapter Ten

MY STUDENTS in Accelerated Sophomore English are easier to teach than my seniors, with the exception of Drake, a tall, quiet, blond boy from Saint Louis who enrolled at the Academy when I arrived. He's in the boarding program but he doesn't pal around with other dorm kids, even though he's handsome and I've seen him in the basketball field house, draining jump shots. He is well read and fiercely intelligent—I can tell from his essay on Vonnegut and Orwell—but he never speaks in class. He sits with his arms folded tight and he won't look at girls who try to flirt with him.

I decide to reach out to Drake. He is a loner here, like I am. Even if I can't reach the wider community, the greater assembly of my students, maybe I can reach Drake. One day after class he stands in the back of the room, looking at my Plurals of Animals poster. It lists phrases giving the funky but correct names for groups of animals: *a crash of rhinoceroses, a smack of jellyfish, an unkindness of ravens.*

"Do you know them all?" he asks. There's challenge in his voice.

"Pretty much."

He tells me to turn around so that I can't see the poster. I do and he quizzes me.

"Ducks," he says.

"Um . . . a paddle. A paddle of ducks."

"Peacocks," he says.

"An ostentation."

"Bears."

That should be an easy one, but I can't remember. I shrug and turn around.

"A sloth of bears." Drake folds his arms and nods at the poster. "Cool list."

"Yeah." I yawn and then apologize for yawning. It's been nine days since I spoke with Mara, and—still unable to sleep more than two hours at a time—I've driven to the lake each night to yell at Lack-of-God. Now I think, *Get out of your head, David, and do something good for someone else . . . then she'll call. Be kind to Drake . . . then she'll call.*

"Your first essay was impressive," I say.

"Thanks."

"Your quotes from *Cat's Cradle* were great. And relevant."

"Thanks."

I ask him if he misses Saint Louis. He says he doesn't spend much time there. It's where his parents live, but he's bounced around the country from boarding school to boarding school for years. I don't ask why, sensing that he's tense about it.

We don't speak for a minute. He keeps his arms folded tight.

I say, "I've been thinking of holding a student trivia bowl, with prize money for the winner. I bet you'd do well. Would you be into it?"

He smiles, just a little. A grudging smile, but a real one.

"Might be cool," he says, and he walks out.

For five minutes I feel not so shitty about myself.

MY APARTMENT is off campus in town, but the other new young Academy teachers have apartments in the campus dorms. These teachers have Dorm Duty: they proctor their dorm students and eat with them in the dining hall. Twice a week the dining hall hosts Formal Family Dinner, where the proctors and kids dress up and eat at white-linen tables set for eight people—one proctor and seven students per table. It's supposed to be a time for civil behavior and sharing wholesome stories, like the Family Home Evenings I used to witness. It's more challenging than the Mormon version, though, because the dorm kids are from Korea, Thailand, Venezuela, the Middle East. English is their second language, but at Formal Family Dinner they have to speak it.

Since I was hired mid-semester, I'm the only new teacher

who doesn't live in a dorm and have a set proctoring schedule. The other new teachers resent this and they really resent that I have an off-campus apartment. They might feel differently if they could see me at three a.m. on my apartment floor, sleepless and nervous and compulsively eating Vlasic pickle spears.

To make things fair, the dorm dean has assigned me to be a floater who fills in as needed for other proctors. When a new female teacher takes a leave of absence, I get assigned to her Family Dinner table.

I show up on a Monday in a suit coat and tie, and meet my seven students. They are three wordlessly polite Thai boys, a Venezuelan girl, and three Spanish kids, two of them girls, one of them a boy. One of the Spanish girls, Annabel, is gorgeous and nineteen—she finished high school in Barcelona and is doing a post-grad year here to get ready for college in the United States. She sizes me up from the far end of the table, while Gonzalo, a confident Spanish junior with badass sideburns, presides over the meal. He passes around family-style plates of pork chops, he flirts with the Venezuelan girl, and then he turns to me.

"Señor," he says, "you walk funny." He imitates with his mouth the clicking sounds that my hip makes.

"I try not to."

He waves my words away. "Señor, I am Gonzalo, from Majorca. You know Majorca? You will come there someday. You must. This food—chops, you say?—this is nothing like what we eat in my island. In Majorca, eating is delightful." He nudges the silent Thai boy beside him. "Hey. Speak to Señor."

The Thai boy looks terrified.

"That's all right," I say. "You don't have to."

"Yes, he does," says Gonzalo. "We all must communicate with each other. It's Family Dinner! Go on, Tong, communicate."

Tong tells me hello. The second Thai boy follows suit. The third Thai boy tells me, "You have nice car."

Gonzalo looks like a proud father. He puts his arm around the Venezuelan girl.

After dinner I have evening Dorm Duty in Larchmont, a three-story mansion that the wealthy, late Larchmont family gave to the Academy. Nathaniel Hawthorne must have designed it. Its top is crowded with turrets and dormers, it has long, creaking staircases, a spooky, off-limits attic, a secret passageway behind the walls, and a stone basement out of *Silence of the Lambs*. Larchmont houses the Spanish and Korean boys, the two most populous nationalities among the boarders.

During Quiet Study Time from seven to nine the boys stay in their rooms, allegedly doing schoolwork. I sit in the drafty main hall at a wooden table under a chandelier, unable to correct the papers in front of me. I stare at a wall portrait of Mr. and Mrs. Larchmont, who built this home.

Did they love You, Lack-of-God? And did You love them? Did they overcome time and distance and other obstacles to be together? Were they ever apart and Mr. Larchmont just flipped the fuck out waiting to hear from the future Mrs. Larchmont?

At nine, stereos come on and the boys pour out of their rooms. The Spanish guys head outside to the Smoking Grotto, which is an area on the back lawn where Larchmont boys are allowed to smoke and flirt with the girls from Beckerman House, the girls' mansion dorm that is across Larchmont Lawn. The guys and girls can't ever go inside each other's dorms.

I stand in the cold on the back porch and stare at the teenagers in the grotto as they laugh and smoke. Drake is smoking alone under a pine tree, while in the center of the grotto crowd are Gonzalo and the Venezuelan girl from dinner. They are communicating by sucking each other's faces. We proctors are supposed to shut down any PDA, but I don't have the heart. I hobble back to the table and correct papers.

An hour later, before lights-out, Gonzalo comes down from his room and sits beside me. The dorm doors are locked now. Gonzalo wears sweatpants and some sort of silky European sleeping shirt. He looks concerned.

"Señor," he says, "you are so sad."

I try to deflect. "What's your girlfriend's name?"

He looks confused.

"You were kissing her in the grotto."

"Oh. Milagros. She's . . . nice."

He asks if I like Quentin Tarantino. He asks me about New York City. The dorm kids know I lived there.

I say, "Hey, I saw Drake in the grotto, too. Do you guys hang out?"

Gonzalo scowls. "I do not like Drake. He is a weird person. You say *weirdo*."

"Maybe he's just new and needs a friend."

Gonzalo waves my words away. "Señor, you will come to Majorca someday? You must. If you visit, you will stay with my family. In my house! In Majorca you won't be sad. There are nightclubs."

I've heard from Daphne that the Majorca kids are from very wealthy families and that they party like gods back home.

Gonzalo fixes me with a probing look. A bolt of pain chooses now to shoot through my hip and ache down my leg. It is a bad one and I shudder.

"Señor, you will love our Majorca nightclubs. There is very little . . . how do you say it, when a girl has never sexed?"

I sigh. He is sixteen. "Virginity," I say.

"Yes. There is very little virginity."

"Okay," I say. "Good talk. Lights out."

He goes back upstairs.

I get home to my apartment late and stand in the kitchen, staring into the fridge-freezer, which I've stocked with frozen Banquet fried chicken, Vlasic pickle spears, and Bass beer. They're my comfort foods. While I'm staring, trying to remember whether I ate dinner at the dining hall, a door in the wall beside me opens. This door is set smack in the middle of the wall, meaning that the bottom of the door is several feet off the ground. I call it the Neighbor Mouse door. At one time there may have been steps leading from my kitchen floor up to it, but not anymore. The door swings open now and my landlord, Ed Neville, sticks his grinning face in. He gapes around until he sees me.

"Schickler! You want a pop?"

Ed is a friendly night owl. He usually has a tumbler of whiskey in his hand—a pop, as he says—and whenever I enter my apartment, the Neighbor Mouse door jolts open a few minutes later and Ed shouts for me and offers a pop. The door is located at the back of his house's pantry, and I can't lock it. Plus I'm living here cheaply, so I try to be a welcoming tenant.

The first time the door snapped open, it scared the fuck out of me, but now I'm used to Ed's Mr.-Furley-like appearances. A couple times I've scrambled up the wall and joined Ed in his house for a pop. But as much as I like Bass, whiskey on a regular basis will make me a full-blown drunk. Also Ed's twenty-year-old daughter, Sarah, lives at home and wears skimpy shirts and no bra underneath them and she is therefore hard to talk to. My first conversation with her went like this:

SARAH: I hear you're a writer. I love Camus.

SARAH'S INSANELY PERKY NIPPLES: Don't look at her, David. Look at *us*.

DAVID: I've only read *The Stranger*.

SARAH: That's my favorite.

SARAH'S INSANELY PERKY NIPPLES: Look at us, David! We also like Camus!

Sarah is dating a guy with a gun rack on his truck, meaning that she's dating a male Vermonter.

I smile up at Ed in the Neighbor Mouse door. "No pop tonight, thanks, Ed."

He asks how my first Dorm Duty was. I say it was all right.

"And how's your hip?"

"It . . . really hurts."

"Hence your need for a pop."

The phone in my living room rings. I say good-bye to Ed and all but sprint to the phone, praying, *Lack-of-God, let it be her, let her love me!*

I pick up and say hello.

"David, it's Dad."

I sink down into a cross-legged position on the floor. My hip crackles and smarts, sharp enough that I see bright white pepper across my vision.

My father hears me catch my breath. "What, your hip?"

I tell him yes.

There's a weighted pause. "Son, I've been talking with Mom. We're wondering if it's time you talked to somebody up there. A psychiatrist. It's just . . . with your anxiety and your hip. They have medicines now . . . mental-health medicines . . ."

The quicksand surges hard, fills my rib cage. *Pills, David?* it says. *Good fucking luck. Do not come at me with pills, kid. I'm stronger than pills.*

"I . . . Thanks, but . . . we'll see, Dad."

After we hang up, I drive to the lake, windows open, gulping in the cold. Once I'm there, I park and pace on the pebble shore, my hip stabbing and cracking, my mind tumbling. I'm exhausted but wired. Five hours from now I have to teach creative writing.

Pills, Lack-of-God? I pray at the darkness. *I don't think so. I think Love, not pills. I think human connection. I think Mara. I need her hands on my skin, not some stranger's hands tinkering with my brain. Please, not that. Please, just Love.*

I GIVE MY SOPHOMORES their creative writing assignment, a two-page fictional story. I tell them that fiction can be real, it can be the truth, even though it doesn't literally happen. I tell them that it can be a lens, a prism, for witnessing and clarifying what's vital in the world.

While I say all this, three girls in my class have little pots of raspberry lip balm on their desks. They dip their fingers into the balm and apply it to their mouths every few minutes. Also their pens have sparkly purple glitter floating in tubes of clear liquid, like handheld lava lamps. Meanwhile two boys stare out the window with fascination at what is apparently the first passing garbage truck they've ever seen.

But not Drake. He sits in the back row beneath the Plurals of Animals poster, with his arms crossed tight, but he's hearing me. Isn't he? He must be, because he's nodding in what looks like agreement each time I say something new about what fiction can do.

He's hearing me, Drake is. He's my hope.

AND THEN the letter comes.

It arrives on a Tuesday morning. I find it in my teacher's in-box in the faculty room, my only personal piece of mail on top of some office memos. The return address says Mara Kincannon and lists a Boston apartment number.

I take the letter to my classroom. My familiar point of pressure throbs behind my right eye. My seniors will arrive for class in a minute and we'll be talking about *The Crucible*, so I tell myself, *Wait, don't open this now, it might say something drastic, wait till later.* I think, *It must be bad news, she would've called with good news.*

I stand at the window. It's a sunny day and light glares off the thick snow on the school's front lawn. In the crosswalk students are bustling between this main school building and Eckhardt, the new school building across Main Street. Even with the windows closed I hear them laughing and swearing at one another as they either hustle or drag their feet in getting to class, and something in the circus of them churning back and forth across the street tells me that maybe the letter I'm holding is the opposite of what I think. Maybe it's a harbinger of hope, of romance.

I tear the envelope open. She has written to me on pale blue stationery:

Dear David:

It was wonderful and confusing to see you last month. I'm sorry that I haven't called, but my plate's been really full and I—

I skip down to the moment-of-truth part, and phrases pop out at me:

... can't see you anymore ...

... part of me will always love you, but I'm in love with him ...

... I think he's the man I'll marry, David ...

... I wish you every great happiness ...

Sincerely, Mara

I put the letter in my pocket and look out the window. My seniors are filing into the room behind me.

Okay, I think. *An answer.*

Outside, there are only a few straggler students left crossing the street. One is Drake, who is loafing, and there's another tall boy ambling along, and the last student is a girl I don't know. She looks like a ninth grader, but she's the tiniest, slimmest one

I've ever seen. She can't be more than four feet tall and the gigantic bright yellow backpack she wears is loaded fat with books. But she is hauling ass, passing the two bigger boys, getting where she needs to be before the bell.

Okay, Mara Kincannon, I think. *Okay. Good-bye. I'm sorry that I dragged you to Medjugorje. I'm sorry that I never got to play Billy Bragg for you. But really and forever, good-bye.*

"Hey, Flatlander," calls out Paul behind me. "This *Crucible*? The girls in it are crazy, right?"

I hear Kira exhale. She sounds impatient with Paul, as she is with all American boys.

"I love this play," she declares.

The bell rings. I keep staring out the window. I know that I'm in my own body, that these are my own tears streaming down my face. But I feel for a second like the pain is someone else's. And there's a chasm between this other young man and me, and I can't reach across it. I can't help him. I can't ordain him, or marry him off to a Kittery knockout, or fix his fucked-up hip. He has to do it himself, I realize. The old me can't rescue him. He has to be a man now, and handle his own shit, and build a life.

"Flatlander?" calls Paul.

The others have stopped chattering. They know something's up. I still haven't turned around.

Paul is the strongest, heaviest guy in the class and I know the sound of him getting up out of his desk. He does so now and steps up behind me.

"Mr. Schickler? You doing all right?"

I pull the letter out and wave it, then stuff it back in my pocket. "I just got some hard news."

"Oh . . ." says Paul. "I'm sorry."

"Thanks." I keep looking out the window.

"Are you crying?"

"Yes."

I hear JoBeth make a soft sound in the background. A mother sound. She and the rest of them can hear what Paul and I are saying.

Paul clears his throat. "Do you need to go home? Take the rest of the day off?"

"You all wish." I sniffle. The ten of them laugh.

"Was it from a girl?" Kira asks. "The letter?"

I nod. They all murmur. This is as invested as I've heard them sound.

I say, "So I just have to get my heart broken to make you guys pay attention?"

They laugh again. It's my first time getting laughs from them.

"Are you going to teach us?" asks Max.

JoBeth shushes him. She walks over beside Paul, behind me. She's been a chatty pain in the ass for weeks, but now she puts her palm on my shoulder. "Mr. Schickler . . . whoever she was, she wasn't the one."

I nod. Inside, I'm still saying good-bye.

Paul pats my back once, then returns to his desk. JoBeth goes back to hers.

I am hurting. I feel empty. Other than my life, I'm not sure there's much left that can be taken out from inside me.

I turn around. "Just give me a second . . . then we'll talk about *The Crucible*."

They groan.

Kira says, "Aw, come on, Mr. Schickler. Tell us about the girl."

They all murmur with assent.

"Yeah," says JoBeth. "It'll help you."

I think, *When Alex Bergeron told me about teachable moments, this isn't what he meant.*

Then I think, *Fuck it*, and I tell them about the girl.

Chapter Eleven

LATER THAT SAME EVENING, I am alone in my apartment, reading my sophomores' creative writing stories. To keep my mind off Mara, I've been sitting on my couch for hours, reading my students' stories and writing comments. Each time I come across a strong, original metaphor or description, I swoop in with my pen to jot down some praise for the writer. I need there to be excellent things in the world today.

The Neighbor Mouse door bangs open in the kitchen.

"Schickler! You want a pop?"

Fuck, yes.

"How about in ten minutes, Ed? I've got one last student paper to read."

"You're on."

The door bangs shut.

I've been saving Drake's story to read last, because I've been so looking forward to whatever this smart brooder might have dreamt up. I'm expecting talent.

I read Drake's piece. By the time I'm halfway through, I'm already bug-eyed. I finish and read it all the way through once again to make sure I really saw what I saw. Yes, I did. I read it a third time to see if it somehow could've been written as a joke, or ironically. No. It sounds earnest, even eager. Worst of all, the writing is carefully and urgently constructed. This is what it says:

One day, I, Fake, got accepted to Fapwood Academy in the state of Fermont. I moved into Farchmont dorm. There were lots of Fanish and Forean boys in my dorm, and the Fanish boys all thought they were the coolest. Little did they know.

My Fenglish teacher, Mr. Fickler, thought he was cool too. But the person who thought he was the coolest was the headmaster, Mr. Fement Fowell. He thought he was hot shit.

I planned. Then one day I was ready. I started with Mr. Fickler. I came into his classroom while he was teaching Fenglish. I had my black-handled Boker magnum lock knife, handmade in Solingen, Germany. Mr. Fickler saw the knife and tried to say "stop!" but I cut off his nose and arms and jammed them all up his ass. I cut off his balls and shoved them in his mouth. Blood poured out of his face and arm sockets while he screamed. All the kids in the class screamed, but I just left.

I went to Headmaster Fowell's office. He had a daughter Faphne, who also thought she was hot shit. Headmaster Fowell was practicing putting golf balls into a drinking glass on the floor. I used my Boker on him. I cut open his stomach and pulled out his intestines and used them to decorate the front of the building like tinsel on a Christmas tree. I rammed one of the golf balls in Headmaster Fowell's mouth and made him eat it.

Then I found the Fanish boys and I used my Kalash-nikov AK-74 assault rifle, 5.45mm caliber, with the 30 mag clip. I shot them all in the stomach so it would take a long time for them to die. That's important. Everyone screamed. There was blood everywhere on the snow in Fapwood.

I finish reading the piece a third time, then I grab the phone and call Daphne.

"Are you okay?" I say.

"Why wouldn't I be?"

My hip is spasming like mad.

"Is Andrew home?" I ask. "And Laura?" Laura is Andrew's daughter from his first marriage.

"Yes, David, they're fine. What's this about? You sound freaked out."

I tell her. Andrew gets on the phone and I tell him.

Then I drive over to Clement's house and give him the essay. He reads it while I stand there in his kitchen. His face flushes a livid red, but he lets himself calm down before he speaks. He asks me exactly what the assignment was. I tell him that I just asked my students each to write a story, to express themselves, to try to get at the truth through fiction.

"Did I screw up?"

Clement shakes his head no. I mention my letter from Mara. He says he's sorry to hear about it, truly sorry. He's not a hugger, but he pats my shoulder once.

Then he holds up Drake's piece. "As for this, I'll take it from here."

I think of Drake smoking beneath the pine tree, all alone. "He doesn't fit in, this kid. I was trying to help him."

"I'm sure you were." Clement's voice is even now, not something to be fucked with. "I'll take it from here."

DRAKE IS EXPELLED the next morning. Clement makes Daphne stay home and away from campus for the day. Drake and his belongings are carted off to the Burlington airport before the end of the afternoon. Drake makes sure to tell the hulking Academy maintenance men who drive him out of Tapwood that his parents will sue the fuck out of the school. This information—and the story of Drake's essay—are everywhere by day's end. At dinner in the dining hall Gonzalo finds me staring at my plate of pierogies. Holding his hand is Swedish Kira.

"Señor," Gonzalo says, "I am sorry for your news."

"Expelling him wasn't my call, but if you'd read what he wrote . . ."

Gonzalo waves my words away. "I don't mean stupid Drake. I am glad he's gone. I mean, I am sorry about the letter you got. Your heart is now crushed."

I look at Kira, and she glances guiltily away. Judging by Gonzalo's grip on her hand, she is his girlfriend of the week.

"Señor, you will come to Majorca, and you'll feel better. It's the best place. The sun, the nightclubs. So happy!"

I wonder if his father runs the island's tourism council.

I thank Gonzalo for his concerns. Then I finish my pierogies and leave.

Late that night, I drive up to the lake. Light snow falls on the dark water and I pray to the God who doesn't exist. But my prayers aren't angry pleading now. They're coming from a deeper place in me than I've known before, a place lower than feeling. They're coming from the Bottom of me, maybe.

Lack-of-God . . . You know that I don't expect ever to hear Your voice now, since You aren't there. And I know that Mara's gone forever, off to another man's bed, to his laughter. And I know that my hip might never heal, that it might hurt and click like a Geiger counter all my life, and that this panic in me might be here for good, too.

But does it really have to be that every person I try to touch or

*teach turns out to be literally disturbed? Melvin . . . Drake . . .
they're dangerously unwell people. Am I too? Is that why I'm
drawn to them, why I try to help them? And why I fail?*

I stare at the water. Snowflakes kiss it one at a time and die.
Ice has formed around the lake's edges and a few peninsulas of
it jut out into the water. Soon the whole lake will be locked
over and frozen white.

I close my eyes.

*Lack-of-God, maybe I asked for all this. Maybe all those years
when I prayed to be pared down and emptied out, maybe I was
praying for suffering, for failure, for Gethsemane. But whatever
this dark place that I'm in is called—holiness or hell—I want to
leave it. Maybe priests and martyrs can love, can actually want
the kind of shit I've been going through. But I can't. To want
heartbreak and pain and humiliation and suffering is madness.
It is fucking crazy.*

My hip twinges. I keep my eyes closed.

*Help me, Lack-of-God. Help me to change now, to be other
than empty. You don't exist, Lord, but help me anyway.*

A WEEK LATER I drive to Montpelier. I'm heading to my first-
ever appointment with a psychiatrist, Dr. Brogan. Clement
helped me find a doctor whose office isn't in Tapwood. I don't
want my students and colleagues to know that I'm a head case.

It's late afternoon and dark out and the panic screams at me the whole drive there. *Never, David, this will never work, I won't let it, you're mine, you're down, you're fucked!*

I play a mix tape to kill the fear. The first two songs are "I'll Fall with Your Knife" by Peter Murphy and "Am I Wrong" by Love Spit Love. I play them ten times each.

The weather outside is subzero. I park in downtown Montpelier and find Dr. Brogan's red-brick office, near the state capitol building. Everything in Montpelier is red brick, quaint, and stately.

I sit in the waiting room, feeling un-quaint and un-stately. Dr. Brogan finally shows me into his office. He is tall and trim with a kind face. He looks about thirty. He looks like he bicycles and stays away from red meat and wants kids.

I tell him everything at once: *I'll-never-be-a-priest-God's-gone-Mara's-gone-my-hip's-fucked-I-never-sleep-Father-Tillermacher-grabbed-my-ass-I-talk-to-a-lake.* I just about chew my fingertips off while I say all this.

"And you're anxious," he says, "about talking to me?"

I nod. I talk about the quicksand. I say that it's in me right this moment, that it's here with us.

He speaks quietly. He says that tragic emotional or psychological events can sometimes alter our brain chemistry. He says that from what I've said, there seems to be a depressive glaze over everything that I do and think about. He asks if that sounds right.

I think about it. *Depressive glaze.* I think of my classroom, my students, myself, all the world coated over with invisible quicksand.

"Yes, that sounds right."

"And how do you feel about medication?"

"I don't want any."

He studies me. "In my profession, we sometimes say that the people who want medication the most need it least, and the ones who want it least need it most. What do you think about that?"

Medication will kill your mind! says the panic. *You'll never write again! You won't even be you anymore!*

"Um . . . maybe I could try it? Just for a while. I don't know . . ."

He tells me about some medicines. I tell him that their names sound Dwarvish, straight out of Tolkien. "You know," I say, "like 'I'm Thorin, in my suit of mithril, bearing the sword of Prozac and the spear of Paxil.'"

He says we should pick a medicine. He talks about different ones. He warns me that for some people the pills make things worse before making things better.

We choose Paxil. He writes me a scrip.

EACH PILL IS PINK and oval with a little ridge down the center. I bring them home and spill them out on a table in my apartment, lining them up. There are thirty of them, thirty strong little dwarf spears planning to poke at my brain and win the day.

I put the pills away. I don't take any. *If I start taking them*, I think, *my failure is complete. It means that I'm giving up self-control, maybe all of my self, period.*

The next evening, the phone rings.

"David, it's Dad. How'd your appointment go?"

I tell him.

"So, you've got some medication now? You've started taking it?"

"Yes," I lie.

"And how do you feel?"

"Better. Yeah . . . I think it's working."

There's a long pause. "David . . . do I need to come up there?"

You've never needed pills, Dad, I think. *Am I that much weaker than you?*

"No," I say.

A couple mornings later I'm in first-period class with my seniors. They're working at their desks, writing an essay about *Lord of the Flies* and *The Crucible*. I've given them a single word as a prompt: *survival*. They're supposed to compose a thesis statement that has to do with survival as a theme, and they have to show with argument and quotes how these books dramatize that theme.

While they're working, Paul and Max, my football thugs, wave me over. Their desks are close to each other's.

"Mr. Schickler," whispers Max, "we'll be thinking of you on Thursday."

Paul nods. "We hope there won't be trouble."

Ever since the letter-from-Mara day, I'm closer with these ten students. But they kid me a lot and I figure this is a joke.

"Why?" I say. "What's Thursday?"

They look at each other.

"Oh, man," Max tells Paul, "he doesn't even know about it."

"About what?" I ask.

JoBeth clears her throat. "Mr. S., they're talking about that psycho kid. Dirk. He's flying back in with his parents and their lawyers. There's a big meeting Thursday morning where you have to defend the assignment you gave Dirk."

"It's Drake," says Kira.

"Right, Drake," says JoBeth.

My stomach has bottomed out. My hip twinges and my head throbs.

"Oh, fuck," I whisper. It slips out.

Kira turns in her desk to face JoBeth. "Can students go to the meeting?"

"No, I hear it'll be closed. Just Schickler and the headmaster and the lawyers."

I go back to my desk and sit down, stunned. *Lawyers, Lack-of-God? Awesome. Why don't You just save Drake the trouble and shove my nose and arms up my ass all by Yourself?*

"How do you guys know all this?" I ask.

Kira shrugs. "Everyone knows. It's Tapwood."

"I'll mess that Dirk up." Max is glowering to himself. He

recently punched his fist through the glass door of the trophy case out in the school's main hall for reasons that I don't know and that he may not know either. He has a month of detention for doing so.

As soon as class is over, I hurry to Clement's office. He confirms what my seniors told me. The hearing will be Thursday morning.

"What am I supposed to say?"

"Just the truth," says Clement. "It's important that you speak. The assignment came from you."

And if I'd never given it, I think, *that boy would still be a student here. Possibly making friends, possibly getting less troubled by the day.*

That night I have Formal Family Dinner. Milagros has transferred to a different table, not wanting to break bread anymore with her ex, Gonzalo, who is also absent tonight because of a field-house indoor soccer game that's running late. The stunning Annabel and her fellow Spaniard from Barcelona, Pilar, sit as they always do at the table's far end, whispering and studying me. My head is rioting with thoughts of Drake, but I spend the meal coaxing short sentences out of Tong and the other Thai boys:

This chicken is good.

America is good.

I talk bad, sorry.

After dinner I have Dorm Duty in Larchmont mansion

again. I proctor Quiet Study Time. A toilet in the second-floor boys' bathroom overflows and I have to clean it up. Finally it's close to lights-out and I sit at the main hall table under the chandelier. When the clock strikes eleven, I'll be free to go home, and the boys will be under the care of their normal proctor, Barry, who lives in the mansion's ground floor apartment, where he spits chaw juice into an old two-liter Mountain Dew bottle.

At five till eleven Gonzalo comes down in his sweatpants and silky sleeping shirt. He collapses in a chair beside me with a groan and tells me that it was a rough soccer game and his squad lost. I tell him that I'm sorry.

"How is your hip, Señor?"

"The same."

He watches me. "I know that weirdo Drake is returning. I know about the meeting. What will you say?"

"I don't know."

"I am sorry that there will be this meeting."

"Thanks. I'm sorry, too."

He looks away and frowns, seeming disgruntled that I'm not confiding in him more. Then his face lights up. "Only six weeks from now is Christmas. Christmas in Majorca! What if you come to stay? For a cheer-up! We will go to clubs!"

I say that flying to Majorca is expensive, and I'm broke. I say that my hip probably wouldn't do me much good in clubs right about now.

His eyes get a sly light. I can tell that he spends a lot of time in Majorca talking to people older than himself, and that he really does go to these clubs.

"Señor," he says, leaning closer, "forget dancing. In our Majorca nightclubs, you will go into the bathroom with me."

I can think of no response to this.

"In the bathroom are many girls. All our clubs are good this way. In the bathroom, you will taste the many girls. The many pussies."

"Oh my God. Gonzalo, we can't talk about this stuff. You're a student, and I'm a teacher. It's . . . inappropriate."

He gives me a startled, almost offended look, as if I've insulted him or Majorca.

"I know you don't want me to be sad. But there are some things that you and I can't—" I feel like I'm telling Hugh Hefner to go do his trig homework. "Listen, you're nice to talk to me. But it's lights-out."

Gonzalo sighs and heads up to bed and I drive home.

THE MIDNIGHT BEFORE the meeting I walk the streets around my apartment. It snowed a full foot recently and the streets are thick and hushed with driven-over snow. The air freezes in my nostrils each time I inhale. My hip hurts and clicks.

I don't see any other people around. A police car follows me for five or six blocks, apparently having nothing else to do.

When I get back to my apartment, I spill my thirty pills onto the kitchen table and line them up again while I drink bottles of Bass. Out the window I can see the Knute Rockne stump.

No matter how big the next day's game, I think, *Knute never needed pills*.

I put all thirty Paxils away.

Chapter Twelve

THE CONFERENCE ROOM has a table with eight chairs around it. At the head sit Clement, the dorm dean, and the Academy's lawyer. Opposite them at the table's other long end is the lawyer for Drake's family. He is lantern-jawed, like Dudley Do-Right.

I sit alone across from Drake and his mother and father. His parents are blond and tall like Drake. Their clothes are Fifth Avenue serious. Their eyes are telling me, *You're young, like our son, don't you understand him?* Meanwhile Drake's eyes, which are golden amber, never leave mine. His arms are crossed tight on his chest.

The lawyers have talked. Drake's parents have talked. They've claimed that his writing was merely inventive, pointing out that the narrator of the story is named Fake, and saying that this clever moniker proves how fictional and divorced from reality the story is. They want their son readmitted to the Academy, or else.

The floor has now been given to me.

"I felt like Drake and I were getting along," I say. "We talked sometimes after class. But then when I read this piece of his—"

Dudley Do-Right interrupts. "What did you tell Drake to write?"

"I told all of the students the same thing. It was a creative writing assignment. I told them each to write a two-page story, to dream up—"

"And that's what Drake did," interjects Dudley. "He *dreamed* his story up. What he wrote is no more an expression of his real feelings than any dream any one of us has is an expression of our real feelings."

Drake's parents nod. I look at Clement, who is looking down at his lap, listening. He needs me to say more.

"Mr. Schickler," says Dudley Do-Right, "you write fiction yourself, don't you? You told Drake as much. You have a *master's* in writing fiction, yes?"

"Yes."

"Well, isn't writing fiction like dreaming?"

I stare into Drake's eyes. They're as golden as hope, but I can see behind the gold. I can see that for Drake there are no lawyers present, and that if there are sweet things in life, they're no concern of his, or at least they're no concern of the part of himself that he's showing me. He wants me to fucking die, period. My hip spasms, jolting me, and the point in my forehead throbs. I suddenly understand that other people's feelings about me and certain pains in me are wrapped around each other like a double helix.

"It's . . ." I look at the lawyer. "It's . . . crafted dreaming. It can't go where you don't steer it to."

Clement nods, without looking at me.

I think of my dad hating my novel, hating where I steered it to.

"But you admit that it's just dreaming?" Dudley Do-Right asks me.

"David is done talking," says Clement. "He's said what he asked for. Now we're going to talk about what he got. I'm going to read what Drake wrote."

Clement proceeds to do so. He reads Drake's whole piece aloud. Then he looks at Drake's parents. "Notice how dispassionate the narrator of your son's piece is. There are no exclamation points in this. Notice how eerily calm and *meticulous* the narrator is as he's *disemboweling* the headmaster of a school who *took a chance* on admitting him even after so many other places threw him out. And which part of your son's piece did you find admirably inventive? The part where he mentioned my daughter disparagingly?"

Dudley Do-Right says, "I don't think we need to—"

"Or the simile where my guts are compared to Christmas tinsel?"

"Again, I don't think—"

"Enough." Clement stands. "This expulsion is permanent.

If Drake isn't off school grounds within the hour, he'll be escorted off."

And then it's over. Drake and his parents and Dudley Do-Right slink out. The dorm dean and the Academy's lawyer leave. I step out into the hall and go to the drinking fountain. Far off down the hall I see Paul and Max lurking in front of the men's room, trying to look like they're just going in or have just come out. They're watching me furtively. I lift a hand in greeting and they raise their chins in acknowledgment.

"Those two of yours?"

I turn to Clement. He's peering off at Paul and Max.

"Um, yes. Two of my seniors."

"What're they doing?"

"I know this sounds crazy, but I think they're . . . getting my back."

Clement puts his hands on his hips and faces the guys, like *Move along, gentlemen, chop, chop.* Paul and Max turn and lope off to class.

Clement watches them go. "Good for them," he says.

Then he looks at me. "David, you can't let what happened in there hit you too hard. There are some things beyond reason. And you have to meet things like that very directly. There's . . . dark shit in some people. Do you get that?"

I DO. I get it. But it's hitting me hard anyway. As I drive the next afternoon to my second Montpelier appointment with

Dr. Brogan, my hands tremble and my breath comes in gasps. There's a line in *The Crucible* about one of the troublemaking teenage girls: *she must be ripped out of the world*. I think of Drake and can't get that line out of my head.

What about me, Lack-of-God? What about things I've done? What about how I am right now? Do I have to be ripped out of the world too?

The quicksand is strong enough that I pull over. I think of Drake off somewhere, buying fertilizer, clock parts, wires, a triggering mechanism. The pulsing point in my temple is making my right eye twitch. I start driving again and I blast Peter Murphy and Love Spit Love.

At the appointment, Dr. Brogan asks how I've been feeling since our first session.

"Still pretty ratcheted up."

"Remember what I said. The Paxil might make things worse first before you feel relief. You've been taking it daily, yes?"

"Yes," I lie.

THE NEWEST BUILDING complex on the Tapwood Academy campus is the Eckhardt Center. It holds classrooms, the dining hall, the vocational culinary school, and the vocational auto school. The auto school runs an actual, three-bay garage business that does oil changes, engine work, and even collision repair for customers from town. In one little-traveled hall of Eckhardt is a large plate-glass window that looks out onto the auto repair bays. If I have a class period free, and my pain and panic are strong, I hide in this hall and spy on the auto students as they fix cars. It can calm me sometimes to see them find a problem—a corroded spark plug or some rusted brake pads—and repair it quickly, swapping in strong new parts, throwing out the old.

On a day just before the Christmas holidays I'm in this hall, trying to get my breath, clenching and unclenching my fists. I've been having nightmares about Drake, and even when I'm awake I see graphic images in my head of him setting off bombs, killing young schoolchildren, studying their corpses with his golden eyes.

He'll be all right, I think now. *He's just young and angry, and that passes. Doesn't it?*

I watch two auto-shop boys put new tires on a Dodge. While they're working, they're talking to a man who, from behind, looks like my father. Then he shrugs in a certain way and I realize that he *is* my father.

I hurry down to the auto bay.

"Dad?! What're you doing here?"

He turns to me. He's wearing a full suit, the way he always does when calling on customers or potential clients. "Surprise, David! Good to see you."

The two student mechanics nod at me, then focus on their work.

"I'm donating some of my fleet maintenance software to

the Academy." My father has grown his company: he now has several employees. He looks around appreciatively at the Academy garage. This is his element. He can take apart an entire car engine and reassemble it. I can't even change a car's oil.

"They've got a great program here," he says, "and I think my product will help them."

I pull him aside. "That's really why you're here?"

He gives me a hug, then stands back, his eyes focusing over my shoulder on a tire balancing machine. "Yes . . . plus, well, you said on the phone how your hip's been killing you while you drive. I figure when you drive home to Rochester for the holidays, I'll just, you know, drive in front of you and run interference. Make sure your hip is up to the haul."

"Dad, you don't have to check up on me."

"I'm here to donate software. Now take me to meet this Clement who's been so gracious to you."

I take him to meet Clement, who arranges for a dinner to be held hours later at his home in honor of my father's visit and his donation to the school. Daphne and Andrew attend, plus Clement and his wife, Beatrice, plus my dad and I. Beatrice makes her chicken piccata over mashed potatoes with carrots on the side. It's a dish she knows I love, and Clement keeps the chardonnay flowing.

My father talks, telling everyone about his business. He's charming and funny and he mixes in stories about growing up on the farm, and all the while my hip spasms and my temple throbs and I drink too much wine. There are candles on the table and from the stereo in the background Handel's *Water Music* plays low, and I want to be taking part in the good event around me.

But sitting across from me, Daphne has never looked so beautiful. She's in jeans and a trim white wool sweater that complements her figure, and she's holding her husband's hand, and laughing at the few things I say, and, *Oh, Lack-of-God, it's too much, it's too hard tonight to look at the other best woman I missed out on. I had chances with her, Lack-of-God. At George-town's graduation ball we slow-danced together—she asked me—and when she visited me in Manhattan once and stayed overnight I almost made a move but didn't. I should've but didn't, I was still too hung up on You.*

I drink a lot more wine.

After dinner my father drives me back to my apartment. He'll be staying a few nights at the Lilac Inn, a bed-and-breakfast near town. He walks me to my door. I have a hip flare-up as I'm climbing the steps and he holds my shoulder to steady me. It's subzero weather again.

"You didn't talk much at dinner," he says.

I think of the cassette tapes in his car. They're tapes of sermons from famous Christian orators.

"David, I can see that it's not easy for you to be around Daphne. She's as gorgeous as you've told me."

"It's not just that . . ." I stare at the Knute Rockne statue. "Dad, when you talk about your work, the fleet stuff . . . you sound like you're in love. You get so excited, and you're an expert and it's your calling and you're inspiring and . . ."

"And what?"

"And I'm not anything."

He makes a small sound in the back of his throat and squeezes my arm. "You're my son. You're my *son*."

"I'm freezing." I turn away from him and go in.

TWO NIGHTS LATER is the Academy faculty Christmas dance. School closed for two weeks earlier in the day and the dorms are empty now. The boarder kids have flown to their home countries for the holidays or else they're spending a fortnight in the States with American friends.

The dance is held in the dining hall, but the place has been decked out in glamorous fashion. There's a huge Christmas tree with white candlelight bulbs and red bows. Actual white candles are lit elsewhere around the room, the overhead lights are off, there's a DJ and an empty, waiting dance floor. Two tables are covered with treats: almond cookies, cupcakes, roast venison on skewers, curried chicken sandwiches. There's a giant punch bowl from which guests can ladle themselves top-shelf Manhattans, Clement's favorite cocktail.

No students or children are present. All the men are in suits and the women are dressed to dazzle. One dark-haired English teacher named Alyssa wears a bold, sleek black dress with matching long teardrops of her abdomen visible on each side, where the material is cut away. Daphne is in a black dress, too. Hers has spaghetti straps, and she wears silver and jade earrings that play elegantly against her hair.

I sit in a corner, drinking a Manhattan, my third. My father is at the food table, sampling venison. He's my date. Tomorrow morning he and I will drive home to Rochester, but right now he's telling Ed Neville—who's having a pop—more about aftermarket auto parts cross-referencing software than Ed will ever need to know. Also listening to my father are Alex Bergeron and his wife, plus Clement and Beatrice.

We're an hour into the party and the DJ has started up the faster music now, trying to goad us all out beneath the silver streamers hung over the dance floor. No one is out there yet, but people are lurking close to the floor, waiting for the party to catch fire. The DJ puts on The Proclaimers and I see Alyssa tapping her feet and nudging her husband, like *Come on, let's groove*, but he's a burly woodsman type who's probably waiting on a ballad.

Daphne keeps glancing at the dance floor too, but she's holding hands with Andrew, who's talking to a tall, older history teacher whom I call Lurch because he looks like the Addams Family character. Lurch is a grouchy, pack-a-day smoker, but both he and spooky Andrew have got it going on over me right now because they're making Daphne laugh, and I'm sitting here alone, hating my flaring hip and my quicksand and my sorry black jealous heart.

"Hey." My father sits down in a folding chair beside me. "I

brought you some venison." He holds out a cocktail plate loaded with treats.

"No thanks, Dad."

He sets the plate down.

"Oh, man." He listens for a second and smiles. "Great song."

It's "I Saw Her Standing There" by The Beatles. No dancers are taking the bait, though.

I nod at my father, agreeing from a clinical distance. *Yes, it's a great song. Yes, venison is tasty. No, I don't want any part of either. I want to sit here like a self-pitying loser and study the pains inside me, for they are me now, and I'm them.*

"Son . . . once we're home, we'll get you back in to see Matt Argento. He helped you before, he'll help again."

I nod vaguely. I think of awful Drake off somewhere doing awful things.

My father makes a frustrated sound. He looks at the Christmas tree, then back at me.

"David."

I know this tone of his. It used to scare the living shit out of me. But now I don't want to hear it. I stare at Daphne.

"David . . . I know you're hurting, but you have to stop acting so proud."

"I think I'm in a pretty humble place, Dad."

"That's not what I mean. You need to start taking those pills."

Jack Sherlock Schickler, I think.

"Maybe," I say.

239

"Not maybe. Definitely. No more screwing around." He waits for a response.

I give none. I'm twenty-five and finally able to be a stubborn dick in front of my dad. It feels terrible.

"So," he says impatiently, "will you? Take them?"

I shrug and look at him. Growing up, I always saw it in his eyes, the dark light that meant I was one split second away from getting spanked or grounded or chewed out. It's there now.

He stands up, looms over me. "Well?"

I shrug again, like there's not a single thing left in the world that could scare or startle me.

But I'm wrong. Because my father starts doing something that I don't see coming. He starts dancing. He backs out onto the dance floor, catching the rhythm of the Beatles song, all the while looking at me with his eyebrows raised like *You drove me to this, sad sack.*

"Well?" he calls once more.

I'm too taken off guard to give an answer, but he doesn't wait for one. He goes into his routine, starting to shuck and jive and boogie, solo-style, like he always does at weddings back home when his favorite songs come on. Except this isn't a wedding back home. This is my new place of work, where people don't know him, and those people are watching him, since he's the only one dancing.

"Hey," I say. It comes out like a complaint and it is. He's too far off to hear me, but he's still looking right at me while he gets down.

"Hey," I tell him. "Just . . . c'mere."

He shakes his head back and forth and then moves it in a beckoning way, like *No, you c'mere.* He stays where he is and keeps hoofing it.

I can see Daphne and others watching my father now. The music switches to "Walking on Sunshine" and I glare at the DJ. He had to pick a barn burner.

I wave at my father, trying to get him to stop and sit. He's in one of his fancier suits and I hope that this will limit his repertoire, but, nope, oh sweet fuck, here he goes, crouching down on the ground and hopping up, doing his famous little explosion move.

I stand, trying to wave him over to me.

Stop. I'm sending him telepathy with my eyes. *You're embarrassing me. Stop.*

Come on. His eyes send me telepathy right back. *Get out here.*

My hip's fucked up.

So dance anyway, his eyes say. *Come on, gimp. One song.*

I see Daphne smiling as she watches him. She makes a surprised face and claps her hands for a second when he does his explosion move again.

God might be a lie, my eyes tell his. *I might never go to Mass again.*

Dance anyway, his eyes say. He does a couple twirls.

I'll never be like you. I'll never be a deacon, and I drink way more than you do, and I can't bear those god-squad preachers whose sermons you listen to. And all the sexed-up, violent books and movies that you hate are all the things that I love and admire and want to write. I can never be good the way that you're good. I can't even want to.

I love you, his eyes say. *Get out here.*

I'm not like you.

You can dance like me. Even better. I've seen it. Come prove it.

No.

I dare you, kid . . .

He's not going to stop.

Screw it, I think, and I slam the dregs of my Manhattan, set down my glass, and go join him. I can't help it. We're probably out there dancing together for maybe only thirty seconds before Daphne and others hit the floor, too, but for those few moments when I'm on show with just him, I bust some crucial moves. I can feel in my hip that I'll pay for this in the morning, but I stomp and glide and whirl alongside my dad. I catch Daphne watching me and looking impressed. It feels good.

I make it through two fast songs, then head back toward my chair, spent.

As I'm going, my dad gives me a thumbs-up and says, "Schicklers can dance their asses off." He has no intention of sitting down.

HE AND I DRIVE to Rochester the next day. Halfway home, while we're at a rest stop on the New York State Thruway, I take my first Paxil pill, being careful not to let my father see. I'm standing outside and looking at brown-slush snow on the pavement. I wash the pill down with some Snapple fruit juice and after I swallow, I wait for some Armageddon in my brain, some revolution in the world around me. It doesn't come. The Snapple tastes like Snapple. The slush looks like slush. The person in my skin is still panicky and neurotic. He's still me.

Chapter Thirteen

"TEACH ME TO DO IT," I say.

It's three days after Christmas. I'm in Matt Argento's office, lying twisted like a pretzel on his chiropractor table while he whales on my hip, cracking it violently, yanking my right leg around. This is my third visit in a week and it's working. My hip pain is less than half of what it was when I left Tapwood.

"To do what?" says Matt.

"Maybe I got my piriformis in trouble this fall because I was stressed out and wasn't going to the gym. But I'm sick of this. The pain. I'm sick of trying to understand it. Whatever you do when you adjust me, it works. Teach me to do it myself."

"Minghia! Mr. Proactive!" He laughs and keeps shoving parts of me around, hard and sure.

"I'm serious."

He stops working, plants his palms on the table, and leans on his beefy forearms. "I'm not an MD, Schickler, but that doesn't mean that you can do what I do. Plus it's a breach of a bunch of—"

"I'm one of your people."

He gives me a level look now, no bullshit. I remember seeing him wear a similar look one time when I was little and we were playing football, and a bully from the next block called Matt's sister a whore seconds before Matt rearranged the guy's face.

He prods my hip with his thumb. "This is really messing with you, huh."

"I feel like I'm ninety. And there's no one like you who I trust in Vermont and I don't want to have to keep coming in here. I'm sick of needing help. Please, Matt."

He studies me for a long moment and nods. "Maybe a couple tips. Off the books."

IT'S MY EIGHTH NIGHT with the Paxil, and it's making my insomnia worse. At two in the morning I get out of bed in my parents' basement and dress and go out to the woods, to the dark path. The snow on the tree branches is Dr. Seuss thick, but my old shadows are where they've always been. I stare at them emptily.

When my hip twinges, I drop to the ground and lie on my left side. I bring my right knee up to my chest. Using my left elbow like a fulcrum, the way that Matt showed me, I wrench my right knee down, cracking my right hip multiple times. I manipulate my right leg around some more, the way Matt showed me, then I hold the right knee down firmly to the ground for fifteen seconds, stretching.

Dear Lack-of-God: I am done crying. Period. And I'm going to end this pain in me. Period.

TWO NIGHTS LATER I meet a girl out for a drink. I haven't seen her in a long time. Her name is Scarlet, she's a couple years younger than I am, and she's the only child of a devout married Catholic couple named Helen and William Cates who live in an upscale part of Rochester called Pittsford and who do Catholic volunteer work with my parents. I'm pretty sure that my mother has told Helen Cates that I'm in a fragile way, and I know both mothers want their children to Meet Someone Nice. Given my frequent quicksand attacks and hip pain and occasional mental whiteouts, I'm not optimistic, but I arrange to meet Scarlet at Richmond's, my favorite Rochester bar. It has a busy downstairs area, but only a few people ever notice the narrow staircase that leads to a grungy, less-traveled second-floor lounge, which has a pool table, old couches, and low lights.

Scarlet meets me upstairs at Richmond's at eleven o'clock one night. She used to be very quiet, now she's very hot. She wears a vintage gray-and-black-striped dress, and black boots, and her blond hair is a bell on her shoulders. She tells me the college in Chicago where she's a junior. Seconds later I've forgotten and I ask her where she goes to college.

"You're so funny!" She laughs and touches my arm. "What've you been up to?"

I decide on the truth. I tell her that I wanted to be a priest, but that that was a bust, so instead I'm taking some really strong antidepressants.

"Wow. Are they working? What do they feel like?"

"Like there's an extra electricity running around under my skin."

"Are you still depressed?"

"Very much so."

Her eyes look more intrigued than when she first came in.

My hip twinges. I say, "Excuse me," and I get down on the floor and pretzel up and crack my hip.

"What're you doing?"

"Adjusting," I say.

She likes doing lemon-drop vodka shots. After she's done her second, she tells me about the classical theater group she's in. After she's done her fourth, she sits close to me on the couch and asks if I want something memorable to happen between us, right now.

I look around. There's nobody else upstairs.

"Yes," I say.

She strokes my left arm and rolls up the sleeve of my U2 T-shirt. Then she leans down and bites my arm so hard that I stifle a scream.

"Scarlet . . . Jesus."

Keeping her eyes on mine, she holds the bite, not letting off pressure. Her teeth are on me for about ten seconds. When she lets up and pulls away, she kisses gently the place where she bit me. She gives me a sympathetic look that seems to say, *I understand all that you're going through, you poor man.* Then she bites me again on the same arm, just above my elbow, just as hard. I again work not to shriek. She holds the bite for a long while, then kisses where she bit me and sits back, looking satisfied.

I stare at my arm. Neither bite broke the skin, but each shows vivid red teeth marks.

"The first bite is you. The second one is me." Scarlet gives me a bedroom-eyes look as if a great wisdom has been shared.

My arm hurts. I angle myself toward Scarlet, hold her, and kiss her mouth. She lets it happen, then wriggles free. She gives me the great-wisdom look again. In confused desperation I try to kiss her once more and I get shut down.

What the fuck? I think. I wonder if this is how courtship works in Chicago or in classical theater groups.

At the end of the night we both go home, separately.

The next morning I'm sitting at the breakfast table with my mother and my younger sister, Jeanne, who is home from college for vacation. We're all eating my mother's blueberry coffee cake, which she makes in abundance for the holidays. My elder sister Pam is in the other room, watching a Christmas movie.

As Jeanne talks about some friends she saw last night, quicksand fills my lungs. I grip the table as the panic shouts,

Give up the pills, fucker! Give up on Dr. Brogan, give up on teaching, so you danced with your dad, big fucking deal, you're alone, you should die!

I close my eyes and try to jolt my thoughts toward goodness. *I'm tasting brown sugar and blueberries. I love this taste.*

You're alone! Just give up, go die, God's a lie, and there's nothing!

There is something, there's this taste, this butter and brown sugar taste. My mother made this and she loves me.

She'll die and you'll die, there's no meaning.

There's this taste. It's real and I love it.

I open my eyes and try to breathe evenly. My mother takes my hand and squeezes it. I take another bite of cake. The spell passes.

But my mother is now staring at my left arm in alarm. She points to the two sets of teeth marks on me. "David, holy cow, did Uncle Nick do that?"

Uncle Nick is our next-door neighbor's dog.

"No ... I went out with Scarlet last night. This, uh, happened at Richmond's."

"What happened at Richmond's?"

"Um ... Scarlet bit me."

Jeanne leans over and inspects my arm. My mother is inspecting it, too. She is a dental hygienist and I was hoping to avoid this conversation, but I forgot to put on a long-sleeve shirt when I woke up.

My mother says, "Scarlet *bit you*?"

"Yes."

"At Richmond's?"

"Yes."

"Were you having an argument?"

"No. We were sort of hitting it off, actually."

"Pam," yells Jeanne, "Scarlet Cates bit David."

My mother runs her fingers over my arm. The teeth marks have turned a deep, wounded blue. "Twice. She bit you twice, I see. David, why in the world did she bite you? Do you know how germy our mouths are?"

"Pam, she bit him twice," yells Jeanne.

"I'm calling Helen," says my mother.

"No. Mom, sit down. It was just a weird moment. I think she thought it was . . . romantic."

My mother is still on her feet, looking at me, perplexed.

Jeanne leans to my ear and asks in an excited whisper if Scarlet and I hooked up. I tell her there were two bites and one kiss and that's all.

"Lord in heaven," says my mother. "Biting people to the point of trauma is romantic now?"

Jeanne laughs. "Trauma?"

"That's the medical term. That's what we say at the office. When skin has been injured to this degree, it's referred to as trauma." My mother is shaking her head. "She did this at a bar. David, no wonder you're so . . . I'm still trying to . . ."

"Did it hurt?" asks Jeanne.

I tell her that it hurt a great deal.

"Of course it did!" My mother points at my arm. "I can see her whole bite pattern, like you took a molding. She should've paid you forty dollars for this. Wait. Oh God, David, did you bite *her*?"

I tell her that I've never bitten any girl.

"And she did it to you twice. So, the second time, you *let her*?"

"Maybe. I guess so. She moved pretty fast."

Jeanne is still laughing.

"David." My mother squeezes my hand again. "I know you're having a hard time right now, but don't let *girls* bite you to the point of *trauma*, okay?"

"Okay," I say.

"I'm getting the iodine." My mother goes upstairs.

"Trauma." Jeanne wears a delighted smile. "Killing me."

CLEMENT TELLS ME to stay in Rochester for one extra week in early January, to work with Matt Argento and keep my hip on the road to recovery. Clement gets a substitute to teach my classes.

I see Matt for three extra sessions, mostly so he can take me down to the gym and coach me through a regimen of stretches, free weights, and Nautilus that I can do in Vermont or anywhere. I am hell-bent on curing my hip. If I can kill the pain there for good, maybe my mind and heart will fall in line, calm down, heal.

Wherever I go, if my hip twinges extra strong, I drop to the ground, pretzel up, crack my hip, and manipulate my leg till the pain is gone. I do it on my parents' kitchen floor, while my sisters watch. I do it on the floor at Marketplace Mall, outside of Banana Republic.

It is something I can do, something I can control, and I don't feel weird about it. I don't care if people see, and I am way past caring what they think. Doing it helps. Paxil can try whatever it is trying in my brain. I am trying this.

MY FIRST WEEK back at Tapwood, I get a membership at the Water Wheel gym. In the fall I did some workouts at the Academy field house, but they don't have the machines that Matt wants me to use, and at the Water Wheel there are no students, so I can focus. The gym is on the banks of the Connecticut River, which flows through Tapwood. The building was formerly a mill, but now it has a workout floor with a big bay window overlooking the river. Since I teach only three Academy classes instead of the standard five, I have two hours free each afternoon starting at one o'clock. I spend this time daily at the Water Wheel staring out at the river while I do my weights, stretches, and hip cracks. I devote myself to my workouts as fastidiously as I once thought I would to vigils or Vespers or other priestly endeavors. When the quicksand invades, I grip extra tightly whichever barbell I'm holding and I pile on the reps. My right calf is still the weakling cousin of my left, but I'm hobbling less, and my hip rarely clicks now.

I still have a mental whiteout once in a while. One morning I find myself walking through a snowy graveyard near my apartment, tracing my fingers over the names on headstones when I suddenly remember that I work at the Academy, and it's Monday, and it's ten o'clock, and I've missed at least two periods I'm supposed to have taught. I walk home as fast as I can, dress for work, drive to school. I go to Clement's office first and tell him what happened. I ask him either to dock my pay or suspend or fire me.

"No. I heard you were AWOL and got someone to cover for you. Just get to your next class." He is sitting behind his desk. I'm standing in front of it and I don't move.

"Go on to class," he urges me.

I wait a moment longer. "Why are you being so nice to me?"

He is focused on paperwork. "Because you're exorcising a demon." He points me toward the door without looking up.

ONE THURSDAY NIGHT I'm assigned to Dorm Duty in Beckerman House, the girls' mansion dorm. It is rare for a male teacher to proctor in a girls' dorm, but lately there aren't enough fill-in opportunities in the guys' dorms, and the other new teachers have grumbled to the dorm dean that I'm getting off easy. So Beckerman's regular female proctor has been given the night off and I'm standing in.

The girls have been told to be on good behavior and I've been told to knock several times on any closed door and announce myself loudly before entering. It's an extra-frigid January night and evening club or sporting events have been cancelled, so all the girls are here. I do a few rounds of the rooms during the first hour of Quiet Study Time and things seem peaceful. Swedish Kira and her roommate from the Ivory Coast, Tanya, tease me and tell me to stay the hell out of their room.

"We're being magical in here," says Kira. "We are *Crucible* girls. Watch your back."

I head down to the basement, which is carpeted over and has three couches and a TV. I correct papers for a while but the couch is too soft and my hip hurts. I lie on the floor, pretzel up, and start cracking.

"Mr. Schickler? What are you doing?"

"Adjusting." I re-angle my body so I can see the doorway. Annabel, the Spanish girl, stands looking down at me, wearing her backpack.

"May I please study down here?"

"It's Quiet Study Time and you're supposed to be in your room."

"*Ay*, my roommate, tonight she is *bip-bip-bip-bip-bip* about boys." She uses her hand to mimic a chattering mouth. "Please?"

"All right. But I have to stretch more."

She sits on a couch and takes out some work. She wears bell-bottom jeans and an Academy sweatshirt two sizes too big for her. She is nineteen and so head-turningly gorgeous that when she first arrived on campus, a male British science teacher hit on her in the dining hall, mistaking her for the new Spanish intern. The man can't be near her now without going crimson.

Annabel looks down at me. When I crack my hip again, she asks, "Doesn't that hurt?"

"It helps me."

She watches me stretch, then smiles. "You make a funny face when you do this stretching. You look like *ornitorrinco*."

I ask what that means.

"You know, this small animal with the funny face who swims. He has a hard mouth, like a duck, but flippity feet and fur and he lays eggs."

"A duck-billed platypus?"

Annabel claps her hands. "Yes. Him. *Ornitorrinco*."

"I'm just adjusting. I don't look like a duck-billed platypus."

"Yes, you do. What happened to your arm?"

I took my sweatshirt off to stretch and I'm just in a red T-shirt. I sit up to catch my breath. The panic comes quick and hard. *The pills aren't working, David, a new gym won't kill me, you're mine, you're down, I fucking own you!*

"Hey," says Annabel, "are you all right?"

I try not to gulp air. To keep the world steady, I focus on Annabel's hair, which is a charcoal-black pixie cut above the permanently sunned skin of her neck.

There's no meaning, David! Hobble off and die!

No. I won't. There is beauty.

"Mr. Schickler? What's wrong?"

It passes. "Nothing." I get up and sit on a couch with my paperwork.

"What happened to your arm, I was asking."

"It happened over vacation." It comes out more snappishly than I'd planned.

"Oh." She looks down at her work and reads.

"I'm sorry if I sounded rude."

She looks at me. It is the appropriating gaze she has aimed my way at Family Dinners.

"I'll bet it's from a girl. That bruise on your arm."

"Annabel."

"Hey, you can tell me. Kira shared with me about your letter. A Dear John, Kira said. I didn't understand that, and Kira said it means a girl destroyed you. In a letter."

"Well—"

"Now you are looking for a new girl, yes?"

"I don't know."

"Mr. Schickler . . . you shouldn't walk around by yourself so much."

I ask what she means.

"I have observed you. When you're with people, you smile, but alone, you are heavy. Sad."

Apparently all Latin people are seers. I tell her that Gonzalo says I look sad, too.

"*Ay*, don't compare me to Gonzalo." She rolls her eyes. "Majorca this, Majorca that. He wrote Kira a love letter with words from this song, 'Let's Get It On,' and he used no quotes. Plagiarism!"

I look down at the papers I'm supposed to correct. It's quiet. If we were out in the real world and I were a normal man and she weren't a student, I'd buy her a drink in this quiet.

"So," she says, "a girl destroyed you?"

I ask her if she grew up Catholic in Barcelona.

"I was raised that way, but I'm not that way anymore."

I tell her my deal. Not all of it, just the priesthood stuff, a couple hints about depression, nothing about sex or pills.

"I see," she says. "So, is this why you have a crush on Ms. Lowell? Because her father is strong in the church and she is too?"

"I don't have a crush on Ms. Lowell."

Annabel gives me a pitying look. "Ms. Lowell is my English teacher, *ornitorrinco*. I see you talking to her."

"We just . . . went to college together."

"And then you lived in New York City, right? Was it so much fun there?"

"You should be doing your homework."

"*Ay*, homework, I can do it in sleep, I get all A's! You're a stubborn platypus!" She pokes my arm with her pen. "You never talk to me at Family Dinner. Talk now. About fun New York City."

I tell her about the Cloisters on the Hudson. I tell her that I miss Chumley's, Hogs & Heifers, the Cowgirl Hall of Fame, the Strand bookstore, St. Patrick's Cathedral, Riverside Park. I tell her that I once went in the Dakota, where John Lennon lived and where *Rosemary's Baby* was filmed. I tell her that I want to write a book that takes place in a building like that, a building that is half the real gritty New York and half fairy tale.

Annabel asks if I'm writing now. I say that I'm not, but I tell her about my Columbia thesis novel.

"Give me this novel to read," she says.

"No way. Well . . ." I have one early thesis chapter with me in my backpack and I pull it out. It is an inoffensive chapter. I tell her that she can read this one part if she wants and I hand it over.

There's a commotion upstairs.

Annabel glares up at the ceiling. "*Ay*, stupid girls! I'm talking to platypus!"

I go up to investigate the commotion. It turns out that one girl called her roommate a fucking bitch and the roommate called her a fucking whore back and now they hate each other forever. I try to mediate a conversation between them, but they don't really need me. They just scream a little more and then they stop and laugh and hug and say that they love each other forever. And then the dorm full of girls goes to bed.

I GO TO THE WATER WHEEL, day after day after day. I gaze out at the river, lift my weights, crack my hip, again and again.

259

I go to see Dr. Brogan. He asks if the pills are helping. I say that I don't know. But I tell him about the Water Wheel and how hard I've been working out. I say that I'm moving my hip toward health, and that if the Paxil is helping me do that, then I'm grateful.

I drive north to the lake late one cold midwinter night. I haven't been coming as often. I still have insomnia, but not as bad as before. I sit on the pebble shore. The lake is a pure, clean sheet of ice now, with the darkness hovering over it. I look into the black.

I'm starting to heal, Lack-of-God. I'm getting stronger. Isn't it sad, though, that the further I get from You and the less often I come here, the stronger I feel? It's sad to me. Of course, if You wanted to do something about that, like, say, if You wanted to decide to exist again, You could. You could choose to exist and to speak just one time, maybe. I'd be all right with that.

ONE DAY I'm lying in the Academy hallway outside my classroom, cracking myself, adjusting. I just finished class with my seniors, and Paul and Max are standing here, teasing me about my stretching.

"You look like a dork," says Paul.

"Yep."

Max says, "You'll never get a chick doing that."

"Thank you, Max."

Daphne's husband, Andrew Preevy, steps out of his classroom, sees me on the floor, and walks over.

"What you're doing," he says, "is not appropriate."

I ask Paul and Max to please head on to their next class. They go.

Once they do, I tell Andrew that I'm not trying to bond with students, I'm just adjusting. I tell him that whenever my hip pain strikes now, I hit the ground and do this, and it's helping.

"You should do it at home."

"Home isn't always where it hurts."

"You have no pride," he says.

I keep stretching. Andrew walks away.

A couple of hours later, at the end of the day, Daphne walks into my classroom. I figure that she's about to tell me to play nicer with her husband, but she doesn't bring him up.

"You're walking better," she says. "Totally normally, it looks like to me."

"Thanks."

She leans back against the wall and gives me one of her cool, easy grins. "So . . . you were a piece of work at the Christmas party."

"How's that?"

"You can really dance."

"I told you about the tutus and all that with my sisters. I hope it counted for something."

She nods. "So, would you like to go dancing sometime? With me?"

"Dancing where?"

"At the Home Run."

The Home Run is a seedy bar in town that has rednecks and a DJ and a great dance floor, from what I hear.

"I don't think Andrew would like that."

"He doesn't really dance much. I told him I'd be asking you."

She's my good friend. But she also has to know how attractive she is to me.

"Come on," she says, "therapy for that hip of yours."

"All right."

"Saturday night?"

"Saturday night."

On Saturday evening I stand in my apartment's spare bedroom, where I keep my clothes. I look around at my outfits. My sisters and mother are forever buying me preppy shirts and ties, but I'm a jeans and T-shirt man. I put on my best non-ripped jeans and a black Ramones T-shirt.

I walk to Daphne's house to pick her up. Andrew's daughter, Laura, lets me in and says Daphne will be right down. Andrew is in the living room, reading what looks like an encyclopedia. He gazes at me over his glasses.

"Hey, Andrew," I say.

He watches me. Other than our weird moment earlier in the week, he's always been cordial, but I'm never sure that he actually sees me. He is a dreamy-headed man and I know what that's like.

"Did you know," he asks now, "that the east–west migration habits of the American black bear are almost identical to those of the Canadian grizzly?"

"No," I say.

He looks disappointed and ducks his head back into his book.

Daphne comes down the stairs and we head out. She's in low heels, jeans, and a silky black top. We're both in sleek coats that aren't warm enough for February, but the Home Run is a short walk down the hill into town.

As we walk Daphne bumps my shoulder with hers. "It's good you're not going to Mass these days. Father Gheritty never plans his sermons. He just walks up to the pulpit believing that the Holy Spirit will tell him what to say. But unless the Holy Spirit is a babbling nimrod who likes to use New England Patriots analogies, I don't think it's happening."

The Home Run is packed. I stash our coats under a table and we each have a drink.

The panic sucks at my heart. *Fuck this night, David! Daphne's not yours, go home to your pickles, the Earth is a doomed cinder in space, and you're unloved.*

Daphne sees my face. "Come on." She pulls me out on the floor.

We're tentative at first, and the quicksand is with me all

through whatever disco-era travesty is playing. Then the DJ puts on "Hippychick" by Soho and "Connection" by Elastica, and the crowd pushes me into Daphne, my hands hold her waist, and there's a melting.

Her eyes ask mine, *Are you going to lead here or what?*

So I do. I lift my hand and she twirls, then our bodies team up close at the hips, and her wrists cross at the back of my neck. I smell her perfume, a light citrus wind, and my hands learn the bones in her back through her shirt.

"You're good at this," she says.

"So are you."

We stomp through "Cotton Eyed Joe" and then groove slow and close to "Crazy for You." I've got sweat at the base of my spine coming through my Ramones T-shirt but she's got sweat at the base of hers, too, and I feel it through her shirt and *Daphne Lowell, Daphne Lowell, why aren't you my wife?*

Eventually my hip acts up, so I have to let go of her body and lead her off the floor. We get one more drink and then leave.

We walk home in the freezing cold. At Georgetown, on the first night I met her, she and I watched *The Shining* together. Now we're walking through a world like the one in that film, a white world walled in by huge drifts.

I get her to her porch. She leans forward and bumps my shoulder with hers. I guess that's our thing.

"Daphne, I . . ." *Forget the expert on bear migrations. Come home with me, I am not all that broken.*

She says, "I had fun, too," then she hugs me and goes inside.

I walk back to my apartment. The Paxil is zinging back and forth under my skin. Once inside, I kick off my shoes and sit upright in the dark on my couch. I don't want to lie down. If I fall asleep now, I might forget how it felt to have her in my arms, and I can't take that chance.

It's one in the morning. Off in the kitchen, the Neighbor Mouse door bangs open.

"Schickler! You want a pop?"

Chapter Fourteen

IT'S THE FIRST WEEK of March now, sugaring season. It's still cold out and there's snow everywhere, but the maple trees are bleeding pleasure by the bucketful. My local-born senior students tell me that they have a surprise for me. They ask me to meet them behind the dining hall after school. I do and they present me with a cereal bowl full of snow. Each of them has a bowl of it, too. Then JoBeth walks grinning out of the culinary school's back door with a steaming teakettle.

"What's all this?" I ask.

"You'll see, Flatlander," says Max.

Paul nods. "A Northeast Kingdom specialty."

JoBeth pours into our bowls of snow what I at first think is steaming coffee but turns out to be fresh, piping-hot maple syrup. The syrup congeals on the snow and makes lumps of confection.

"What do I do?"

JoBeth says, "You eat it, duh. It's called sugar-on-snow."

"You're supposed to have pickles and doughnuts with it," says Paul, "but someone flaked out."

Max punches Paul.

"I love pickles," I say.

JoBeth tells me to shut up and eat, then we do. We snack on what they all grew up on. It's delicious.

DAPHNE SITS DOWN next to me at lunch one day in the dining hall. She is dressed sharp in a suit. She'll be going with her father on a trip later in the day where they'll attend a meeting in New Hampshire to talk to people about the Academy or recruit students or something.

"So," she says. "Guess what's coming up in May?"

She informs me that there's an annual school event called Spring Day where the students get the day off to play games outside and compete by classes, juniors versus freshmen and so on. There's Ultimate Frisbee and dunk tanks and revelry. The best part, Daphne says, is that at the end of the day all the students gather on the hill near Larchmont grotto and watch the faculty square off, department versus department, and battle one another in various competitions, sack races and other embarrassing stuff on Larchmont Lawn. She says that the faculty departments take it seriously because they want the year's worth of bragging rights and lording it over their rival disciplines. She says that the English department hasn't won in many years, and she also says that the final, most heavily scored and popular category in the competition is a dance contest.

"And?" I say.

"And I'm entering you and me, representing English."

My hip has been getting better and better. Daphne and I have had a couple other Saturday dancing nights at the Home Run in the past six weeks and I'll be able to recount, if the FBI or alien interrogators ever ask me, exactly what Daphne wore on each of those nights and what she drank and what I said that made her laugh and vice versa.

"I want you to choreograph it," she says now. "And I want to tango."

During my first semester at Columbia I took a few ball-room dancing lessons as a lark and I've told Daphne about them. I've told her that I didn't go for most of it, but that I loved the tango. When she asked why, I said that the tango is basically a man and a woman having sex with their best clothes on, while they dare the whole world to watch and have a problem with it.

I look down at my turkey tetrazzini. The panic says, *She's kidding, David, it's a joke, get this through your fucking head, you ARE NOT WANTED!*

"You want to tango with me," I say.

She nods. "And we're not going to tell anyone about it until we spring it on them at the contest, and we'll practice in secret, and you'll choreograph it. You're going to be my Mr. Roarke, okay? I want that victory, David. Don't even think about saying no. Say yes."

I see Annabel at a table in the distance, watching us.

"Yes," I say.

I SIT ALONE on the lakeshore at two in the morning, staring at the darkness. The ice on the water has started breaking up.

I keep my mind clear. I don't pray to Lack-of-God, and I don't petition the night. The air is frigid good. Some animals scuttle in nearby branches. It's been six days since my last quicksand attack, a new record.

I think of my father. One summer when I was a boy, the rhubarb along the edge of our backyard didn't grow in. I was upset because I wanted to chew the sweet stalks. I asked my former-farmer dad what I could do to treat the ground, to bring the rhubarb back.

"Nothing much," he said. "When soil is fallow, it's fallow."

He told me you can fertilize a little, maybe, but that you can't shock fallow ground back to life. It either gets rich in nutrients again on its own or it doesn't. You have to leave it be.

I HAVE DORM DUTY again in Beckerman House on a Tuesday night. I make the rounds twice during the first hour of quiet time, checking to be sure the girls are in their rooms, studying.

Kira and Tanya hide from me each time that I come around. The first time they are wedged behind their bureau, stifling giggles. The second time they bring their A game and after a couple full minutes of searching I get frustrated. They emerge laughing from inside Kira's leather-bound footlocker.

"How'd you ever fit in there?"

They scrunch back down in and twist around each other, then close the lid.

"I told you," the footlocker says, laughing. "We're *Crucible* girls. Don't screw with us."

"Come out and study."

The footlocker sighs.

Kira pops the lid and rises up. "Boring," she scolds me.

Later I knock on Annabel's door and poke my head in. She asks me for help on the English paper she's working on for Ms. Lowell. Each student has to select a poet to read and critique, and Annabel is doing e. e. cummings.

"Let's talk in the common room, please," I say.

She follows me down to the basement. We sit on a couch and she shows me the e. e. cummings poem "in Just-." She says she likes it because it is about now, about spring, her favorite time of year.

"And I know," she says, "that this goat-footed balloon man who whistles far and wee, he is Pan. From mythology! And I will write that. But the rest of the poem is so simple, I don't know what else to say."

I tell her there's a potential double entendre in the word *wee*. I tell her it could be a noun, and that *we*, the readers, are maybe being invited into the poem and being asked what we will do in spring, when Pan whistles for us to follow him.

"Clever platypus!" She jots notes. "Hey, you walk correctly now. I have observed you. Congratulations."

I tell her thanks.

"But," she says, "what is all this at the Home Run? You and Ms. Lowell?"

I blush. "How do you know about that?"

"*Ay*, this is Tapwood. Everyone knows."

"We just dance."

"You think about her too much, *ornitorrinco*. You have to get her out of your system so you can meet a girl."

"Go upstairs. Work on your paper."

"No! We are talking!" She puts her poetry project into her backpack and pulls out the first chapter of my thesis novel. I'd forgotten that I gave it to her.

"This is good." Annabel passes me the chapter. "But it has too much sadness. Can't it be funny and sweet, too? You are these things. When you write your New York book, you must make it funny and sweet."

I tell her that if I ever write it, I'll try. I ask her if she's sure her name isn't Esmé.

"I do not understand this question," says Annabel.

"Never mind. Go work on your paper."

———

I BUY SOME TANGO CDS at a record store in town. I listen to them alone at home and finally select an instrumental recording of "Por una Cabeza," the tango music used in the films *Scent of a Woman* and *True Lies*. The original version of the song, a hit from the 1930s by Carlos Gardel and Alfredo La Pera, was about a man as addicted to the beauty of women as he was to the horses he gambled on. The music is addictive too—a strong, clear violin and piano arrangement—and I play it for Daphne and she agrees that it's the one for us.

Late at night now, instead of driving up to the lake, I move the furniture aside in my apartment and I choreograph a routine. I rent and watch *Scent of a Woman* and *True Lies* for tips. I'm not my sisters, and I don't have much tango experience, but I know how it's felt all my life to stand close to Caitlin and Lesley, to Sara Draper, to Audrey Vaillant, to Sabine, to Annabel, to Mara, to Daphne. I try to put all those feelings in the movements. I keep the music low so Ed Neville won't barge through the Neighbor Mouse door and catch me dancing with myself.

For our first rehearsal, Daphne and I meet in her classroom at school one evening and draw the blinds. There's no one else around and Daphne told the maintenance guy not to disturb us, please.

I play "Por una Cabeza" for Daphne. We watch the *Scent of*

a Woman tango scene on a classroom TV and VCR set. Then I show Daphne what I've come up with and we try it. It's awkward at first, at least for me, because there's no loud, anonymous crowd around us like at the Home Run. Daphne holds me close, the way I show her to, but our movements are too mechanical, too stilted, too borrowed from things I've seen other dancers do.

My chest softens with fear. The quicksand is percolating.

"David, we'll get it," she says.

IN MID-APRIL, Barry, the regular live-in proctor at Larchmont dorm, is given a weekend off duty and I'm scheduled in his place. This means that I'll stay in his ground-floor apartment for Friday night and Saturday night and I'll watch over the Larchmont boys full-time.

Friday night starts off fine, with the boys behaving themselves at dinner in the dining hall. Then we head back to the dorm and I play Ping-Pong with a few Thai kids. They annihilate me.

Around eleven the real nightlife of Larchmont dorm reveals itself. The Korean boys walk around in tighty-whitey underwear without shirts or socks. I smell marijuana somewhere but can't locate the source. I hear cacophony in the basement and head down.

"Hello?" I call. The basement has cement walls and floors, with nooks and alcoves off a main hallway.

"Ladies and gentlemen," says a voice, "what did the Larchmont boy say to the Beckerman girl on the chaperoned trip to the bowling alley? 'Check out my blue balls.'"

There's a bah-dump-bump of drums, then a cymbal clash.

"No, seriously," continues the voice, "you're a great crowd."

I come around a bend into the basement's large main room. There are laundry machines in one corner and in an opposite corner, inexplicably, is a full drum kit set up beside the mossy, crumbling cement walls. Behind the drums is a Larchmont student named Henry, and standing in front of the kit, holding a broken broom handle like it's a microphone stand, is Henry's roommate, Phillip. There's no one else in the basement. They're both in sweatpants and T-shirts, but Phillip wears a porkpie hat. When he sees me, he grins, holds a hand toward me, and speaks to an imaginary audience.

"Folks," he announces, "it's David Schickler, from the great city of Rochester! Mr. Schickler, welcome to the show! We're the Catskills Boys!"

"Guys," I say, "what the hell?"

Phillip struts around like he's onstage and talks into the broom handle. He and Henry are in the Academy theater group.

"Ladies and gentlemen," says Phillip, "Schickler here got off to a rocky start last fall because of his bum hip. But now he and the Academy are really 'clicking'!"

Henry does a rimshot on the drums.

"Clicking." Phillip arches his eyebrows. "'Cause of how your hip used to sound."

"I get it. Please don't drum so loudly. I'll give you a half hour, then it's lights-out."

I head back to the stairs.

"Come back for our midnight show tomorrow!" Phillip calls.

When I do room inspection before lights-out, one large Korean boy, Kwan, has left his room a mess. For punishment—which I've been told I have to give—I tell Kwan to take the trash barrels off each of the mansion's three floors and empty them out in the Dumpster. He nods dutifully and heads off to the third floor.

Minutes later I'm on the ground floor and I see a tiny Korean boy, Hyo, come downstairs struggling under a huge, full trash barrel. I ask him what he's doing.

"Sheeklah, I am help Kwan. My friend." Hyo looks nervous. I let him go empty the barrel, but I walk up to Kwan's room to ask what's up.

"A mistake, Sheeklah. I will take care of it. Sorry, Sheeklah."

The next morning in the dining hall, the dorm dean pulls me aside. "David, Hyo spoke to me. You can't punish Kwan or his roommate Shin unless you watch them carry the punishment out."

"Why not?"

"Because of the Korean mafia."

I wait for him to say more.

"That's just what some of the Korean boys call it," explains the dean. "They have a carefully worked out hierarchy among themselves. Shin is president, Kwan is the enforcer, the rest are drones. When punished, Shin or Kwan will delegate their work to a drone."

"Are you being serious?"

"Yes." His face is earnest.

"Hyo is a drone."

"Yes."

"All right, I'll talk to Kwan again."

"No, Hyo probably already got beaten up once for letting you catch him emptying the trash. Best just to let this one go and be more careful in the future."

"Yes, sir," I say.

As he's walking away, I hear an odd, unfamiliar sound. I realize that I'm laughing.

WE'RE IN DAPHNE'S classroom at night again with the blinds drawn. "Por una Cabeza" plays quietly from my tune box in the corner.

We're both in jeans and T-shirts. I move her back across the floor. When I raise my hand, she improvises, striking a saucy, preening pose with her head thrown back and her chin lifted.

"That's perfect!" I say. "You've got to keep that in."

She nods and we tango on, looking into each other's

eyes. I'm holding her close. I'm wanting to hold her ten times closer.

"David," she says, "when you get grooving, you get a sneer on your face. That's so tango, you've got to keep that."

I hold her and dip her toward the floor, a little conservatively.

She makes a chiding sound. "Come on. Go for it more."

She has no idea how far I'd like to go for it. Or more likely she does, but is too classy to say.

I dip her further.

I'M SLEEPING BETTER. I don't have mental whiteouts anymore. It's been three full weeks since my last quicksand attack. Dr. Brogan tells me he thinks it's the pills. I think it's one part the pills, one part sugar-on-snow, and three parts the tango. But I keep this to myself.

One morning in my classroom while I'm teaching my seniors, I hear a loud sound that I think is wailing. JoBeth is reading aloud a Shakespeare sonnet and I ask her to keep reading to the class while I go check what's happening. I walk into the hall and follow the sound of human misery. But it isn't misery, it's laughter, coming from Daphne's classroom.

I go in and she's sitting behind her desk, with her hand covering her mouth. It's a free period for her and there are no students in the desks. Daphne is crying because she's laughing so hard. Her face is bright red. When she sees me, she starts pointing wildly toward a paper on her desk. She can't get enough air to talk at first, but she grabs the paper and holds it out to me.

"Oh my God," she gasps, "read it, read it. It's not a joke, it's poor Missy Turner's actual paper. Oh my God, David, oh my God."

I take it and read. Whimpering laughter, Daphne reads over my shoulder. The paper begins:

POETRY PROJECT TOPIC: SYLVIA PLATH
BY: MISSY TURNER

Sylvia Plath was an American poet and wife who killed herself by shoving her head into a front-loading washing machine, while it was running.

Sylvia hated being a wife and mother. She was depressed. One of her poems, "Childless Woman," is really powerful. She compares herself to a huge spider!

Sound crazy? Remember: Sylvia killed herself by shoving her head into a front-loading washing machine, while it was running.

I'm laughing as loud as Daphne. She's leaning on me, still crying from laughing, and waving a hand in front of her face to swat away the absurdity.

JoBeth appears in the doorway. She shakes her head at the sight of two indisposed adults.

"Come back now," she tells me. "We need you."

A COUPLE WEEKS later the Academy community is dealt a horrible blow: Tanya, Kira's roommate, dies unexpectedly of a brain aneurysm. There are no warning signs, it simply happens.

The day it is announced at school, all gatherings and conversations have a pall over them. JoBeth, who knew Tanya well, weeps steadily during English class. Kira is absent. I ask JoBeth if she wants to go home to be with her baby, but she says that she needs to be here with us.

I try to wear a strong face, but Tanya's death shakes me as much as the students. There are flutterings of pain in my hip. After school I go down to the bookstore in the Academy's basement and hide between two high shelves. I close my eyes and breathe in and out slowly. I lie down, crack, adjust.

Lack-of-God, this is no time for games. Come back and exist for the sake of this girl. Make heaven real and bear her up to it.

Kira is devastated and won't leave her and Tanya's room. For days she stays in Tanya's bottom bunk, wrapped in Tanya's sheets. She can't be consoled and will not be pulled free.

The tragedy hangs over all the campus, and all our hearts, for weeks. Then May comes and the weather won't stand for sorrow. The sun softens up Larchmont Lawn, the sky is clean blue parchment, and deep rills of runoff water come down the hillsides near school as snowdrifts melt. Birds and tree buds pop with songs and colors, and the clear mountain air is just shy of sixty degrees.

Early one Tuesday morning I have Dorm Duty in Larch-mont. I hound all the boys out of the mansion, send them to the dining hall for breakfast, lock the dorm so they can't get back in till after school, and then do morning inspection of their bedrooms to see whether demerits need to be doled out. The mansion is eerie and quiet as I make my rounds, but all the boys' rooms look clean, which is a nice surprise. I'm on the ground floor about to leave for school when I hear a thump upstairs. I go back up and investigate, looking more carefully in all bedrooms and closets.

When I get to the room shared by Tong and another Thai boy named Kanda, I hear breathing. The room is spotlessly neat—the Thai boys' rooms always are—but at the foot of Tong's bed, there's a person crouched inside his wastebasket. It's a fairly large wastebasket, wide and over two feet tall, and the boy inside is small and tucked down with his hands over his head, trying to hide, but his back is still protruding out in plain sight. I tap his back and he doesn't respond.

"Hey. Lift your head up." I tap him again and he finally looks up at me. He's not Tong or Kanda. He appears to be Thai, about sixteen, but he isn't an Academy student. He beams at me as if we've been friends forever.

"Who are you?" I ask.

"Oh . . . is okay, I am Pu. Friend of Tong. I stay here while Tong is at school. Is okay, no problem." He tucks his head back down inside the wastebasket as if our business has been completed.

I tap him again and he looks up.

"How'd you get here, Pu?"

He chews his lip as if deliberating. "I am from Bangkok. I fly to New York and come here on bus last night. A visit. I am friend of Tong, is okay, no problem, don't say things about me, I stay here while Tong is at school, okay?"

He makes no move to get out of the wastebasket and I realize with something like eternal delight that if I tell him that he may stay here hiding in Tong's wastebasket all day long, he might actually do it and might feel somehow victorious about it. This thought throws a party in my brain.

I'm happy, I suddenly think. *Right here, in this place, I'm happy.*

"Let's go, Pu. I have to take you to the dorm dean now, so we can figure out what to do with you."

"Is okay, mister teacher. I just stay here."

Through my laughter I say, "Pu, get out of the goddamn trash can right now."

SPRING DAY is almost over. The students have had their fun, their sports, their water wars, and now they're gathered in droves on the hill near Larchmont grotto, sitting and watching the faculty interdepartmental competition on the lawn below. The teachers have done three-legged races, egg tosses, and tricycle races. Daphne and I have stayed out of all these. She and

I are hiding in Larchmont mansion, watching it all from the window.

Daphne is in a scorcher of a black dress that ends at her ankles. I'm in a black suit. We're both barefoot, because I told her we can't take a chance on one of her heels or my shoes coming off in the slightly muddy grass we'll be dancing on. It would ruin the moment, I said, and she agreed.

Annabel zips up the hill through the crowd of students. She ducks inside the mansion through the back porch and finds Daphne and me. She is our accomplice.

"Only the dance competition is left," she says. "English is behind Math by five points and behind History by three. For a victory, you must take first place in dance."

"Thank you," says Daphne.

Annabel nods. She pulls me aside.

"Thanks for helping," I tell her. "Not just today."

She smiles. "Good luck, *ornitorrinco*." She glances at Daphne, gives me one quick kiss on the lips, then scurries outside and back down the hill.

I go to Daphne and we watch out the window. A large stereo system and speakers have been set up under the pine trees so the music is loud. Math teachers do the twist along to the Chubby Checker song.

"I'm crazy nervous," says Daphne.

I tell her, "I'm swallow-my-tongue nervous."

"Can I borrow like ten Paxils?" She squeezes my hand.

Two history teachers do the hustle and the kids cheer.

"Dammit," Daphne says. "The kids are loving History."

I remember my cross-country meets in high school. I couldn't eat in the morning before races and I haven't eaten yet today. My stomach is storming the Bastille.

The hustle ends.

"Ready?" I ask.

Daphne shakes her head no.

I take her hand and we walk out of the mansion. We move down the hill through the throng of kids. As they turn and see how we're dressed, they start hooting and catcalling.

"Sheeklah!" calls Kwan.

"Ms. Lowell!" calls another student. "How 'bout some hip-hop, Ms. Lowell?"

Daphne throws her shoulders back and raises her chin, like the first-class act she is. We step down through all the rowdies and take our place in the sun on a clearing in the trammeled grass. I pull Daphne near. She arches her back, resisting me like she should. Holding each other this way, we stay still.

Gavin, the history teacher who hustled and who's wearing a Hawaiian shirt, calls out, "What's this fancy crap?" The students laugh.

Daphne and I stay still and wait. Her right hand holds my left. I have my right arm around her waist. The violin of "Por una Cabeza" begins, gentle but loud through the speakers.

I move forward at Daphne and she steps back. There's a slight splash of wet from the grass beneath our feet. We move with the rhythm, holding each other at bay with tension in our arms. There is still air between our bodies and not much danger yet.

"Too slow," complains a student.

"Yeah," says another.

The violin climbs higher. I look deep into Daphne's eyes.

Her expression is aloof, pouty, and inviting at once. *If you want me, prove it.*

I will. On the piano's four-note solo flourish, I thrust her away and reel her in hard. Our torsos crash together and the crowd gasps and cheers.

And that's the spark. We're off. Our bodies move like a shared fate over the lawn. I've never held her tighter. The violin is a heat between us and the piano notes are little cracks from a whip at our feet. The crowd might still be here, nearby, but I wouldn't know it, because Daphne's breasts are against my chest, her legs move with mine, and our eyes are locked together, having a once-in-a-lifetime pillow talk.

This is as close as I'll ever get to you, isn't it, Daph.

Yes.

We'll never kiss and we'll never make love, will we.

No, David.

You're not my wife.

No, I'm not. But just for this moment, for this dance . . .

I dip her so close to the ground that her hair teases the grass. Then I whip her back up, grip her tight, and tango forward. The music keeps on, moving toward crescendo. Our foreheads are touching and our eyes stay each other's. Somewhere it is night right now, and the stars are candles, but behind that light, rolling in the darkness, are all the world's lovers.

I don't know who she'll be, Daph, but I'll find her.

I know you will.

I'll write my way toward her.

You should.

That's my path.

Then let's tango.

We make one last-ditch pass over the grass, really flying now, improvising. I sneer the way she wants me to. Still clinging to me, she flounces her head side to side with a strict, pert grace. We dash down past the crowd and I see each drop-jawed face, Gonzalo's, JoBeth's, a smiling Kira's, and then glad, glad Annabel's. I see Paul and Max punching each other and grinning and pointing at me. I see Clement looking happy, watching his daughter.

Leaping onto the trammeled mark where we started, I stop my feet and strike a pose, with one foot extended out into the mud. Daphne sylphs her body around mine, adding one final intimate glimmer, then stretches out a leg to match and cleave close to mine. As her toes touch down softly to the mud, the music ends.

The crowd leap to their feet. They go crazy with ovation.

She and I are panting, still gazing at each other.

"We just won," she says.

Chapter Fifteen

FIVE YEARS GO BY. I teach full-time in Tapwood for two of them, then I move back to Rochester and teach English at an independent high school. To give myself a chance to write, I teach only half-time and to afford this, I live in my parents' basement again. I stay on the Paxil. As long as I stretch and lift weights, my right hip stays mostly out of pain. I can run again and I do so around the grounds of Black Creek Country Club and on the dark path, though I have a hitch in my gait now and my right calf will forever be a slimmer, atrophied version of my left.

Quietly and usually alone, I start going to Mass again. I go to Holy Ghost Church on Coldwater Road, near my grandparents' old farm. They are buried in the churchyard cemetery. After Mass I sit in the grass by their graves. In church, in the graveyard, and on the dark path, I mostly just show up, attend, rather than petitioning. What I feel now in the shadows around me on the path, and occasionally in church, is that I'm hovering, caught, between God and Lack-of-God. I feel both His presence and His absence. I can't break out of this paradox or dilemma. I also can't articulate it, so I don't speak of it.

Instead I write fiction, every day. I throw myself into it. I try writing a novel about a spiritual little girl. It has sweet parts, but overall it doesn't work. I try writing an erotic novel. It has hot parts, but overall it doesn't work. Then I write my New York book, a love letter to the city, and it works. I call it *Kissing in Manhattan*. It features a short story called "The Smoker," a story inspired by Annabel but not based on her, and "The Smoker" comes out in the *New Yorker*'s summer fiction issue, and, incredibly, I get a book and movie deal. The deal is strong enough that I can stop teaching and write fiction and screenplays full time. It is the heady summer of the year 2000—my thirty-first summer—and I can barely drive my car because my hands keep shaking on the steering wheel, not from panic this time but excitement.

In late September I do my first-ever reading from my book, at Geva Theatre in Rochester. At the cocktail reception afterward, a young woman introduces herself. Her name is Martha. She is a tall blonde with a killer figure, a shy smile, and deep brown eyes. There's a crackle in the air between us. She says that she came to the reading alone, on a lark, after seeing it advertised in the paper. She loves horses and owns one and her eyes dance when she speaks of him. Martha comes out for a drink with me afterward and we kiss good-night leaning against her car. There is a scent to her neck skin. It is sweet and addictive, like warm vanilla something-or-other. We go out days later and she's wearing a cool leather jacket and she still has that same scent. It isn't a perfume. It's her.

I try not to think too much about Martha, though, because of My Plan. My Plan—which I devised ten seconds after I got my book deal—is to move down to New York City, the East Coast mecca for hotties. In Tapwood and since, I've had full-on sex with just two women and both times were mistakes. For whatever reasons, Catholic or neurotic, I simply can't have complete intercourse until I'm married. But I feel skilled in the Everything But department, and *Kissing in Manhattan* is racy and romantic, and I want to use it as a calling card. I will be Hip and Racy Author David, and My Plan is to urge my book into the hands of ten thousand young women in Manhattan and let my writing melt their hearts and hopefully their clothing, too. I will take these ten thousand women to bed, one or two at a time, and get to third-and-a-half base with each of them. In my own Catholic, premarital way, I'm going to get repeatedly and spectacularly laid.

In early October, I try to put My Plan into action. I drive down to Manhattan for a week to sign a lease for an apartment on Riverside Drive and to read a story from my book at a cocktail party that *The New Yorker* hosts for me at the Polo store in SoHo. At first I think it's weird that the magazine is partnering with a fashion store for a literary event, but then I remember that I am Hip and Racy Author David and whatever happens is cool, baby, cool.

It is a dream-perfect evening, this cocktail party. I read my story and people laugh. There are dream-perfect hotties in attendance, smart, stylish young women who work in publishing and fashion. One is a six-foot-tall African-American girl named Plesha, who is wearing a silver shift and who loves the films *The Warriors* and *The French Connection*, like I do. Another woman, a raven-haired Jewish fiction editor with a soft laugh and an Akris Punto drape-front dress, smiles at my dumb jokes and asks if I'd like to go sometime to Chat 'n' Chew for mac and cheese.

Both women give me their numbers and both seem to be what I'm looking for, sheer, wild, brilliant Manhattan hookups waiting to happen. The editor smells like the sweet red wine she's drinking, and Plesha wears a perfume that smells like cinnamon danger. But neither of them smells like Martha, the vanilla woman I left upstate. Goddammit.

I drive back to Rochester, just for a few days, to get my stuff, and while there I have another date with Martha, then another, then another. She keeps kissing me and smelling all vanilla-ish. She is ruining My Plan.

When I move to Manhattan, Martha visits every other weekend and stays with me. I tell her that when she's away, I will see other women. But I never do. Instead I call Martha every night that we're apart.

We make no sense together. Billy Bragg led me to expect a brunette, and Martha is blond. She doesn't drink. She's an erratically practicing Protestant. I'm a night owl, but if we go to an eight p.m. movie, she is out cold on my shoulder by half an hour in. The more crowded a room gets, the louder and gladder I get, but if I want Martha to make a peep, we can't go out to dinner with more than one other couple. Her family is tiny. When I tell her that I have fifty-four first cousins, she lies down on my apartment floor, dizzy and terrified.

I love trivia. One night when we're walking down Broadway I ask Martha which U.S. state contains the geographical center of our country. She crosses Broadway to look in a shop window. I follow her, thinking that she must not have heard me. When I ask her the same question, she turns away from me to a street kiosk and buys some mints.

I ask her what's going on.

"I don't like being wrong," she says.

When we're at bars with dance floors, I try to pull her out there with me. Almost every time, she's having none of it.

One night we're sitting in the lobby of the New York Palace hotel. Attached to the hotel is Sirio Maccioni's swank restaurant, Le Cirque 2000, where my younger sister, Jeanne, is a cocktail waitress now to support herself as a modern dancer here in the city. Martha and I are about to go in and sit in Jeanne's section and gawk at the upper crust, but first I've pulled Martha aside here in the hotel lobby to tell her for the first time that I love her.

She goes pale. "Oh, God. Please don't say that just because I need to hear it."

I promise her that I mean what I'm saying. She hugs me close and says that she loves me, too.

I DON'T LIKE being wrong any more than Martha does. And about her I can't afford to be. Because when we're in bed and she's asleep beside me, she smells not just like vanillaness but foreverness. Somehow her warmth and kisses are making me need God not only to be real but to be eternal and willing to share His eternity with the two of us. This simply has to be the case and I don't know what to do. I've long since given up on expecting God to speak to me, but I need Him to be irrefutably there. I don't know why, but I need to know He's there before I can ask her The Question.

I turn to my father. Over the holidays home in Rochester I help him decorate the outside of our house for Christmas. I give him a hand putting up Tannenbaum pine trees on the back deck. While we're out there in the snow, stringing lights on the trees, I ask him when he knew that my mother was the one. He smiles and grimaces as he works.

"Well, my dad, your grandfather, never said much about anything. But I brought Peggy out to the farm for dinner one night, and the next morning while Grampa and I were fixing his truck radiator, he said, 'Jack, don't let her go.' Then he asked me for the socket wrench."

I nod. I'm trying to untangle strings of lights from out of last year's wooden bins. Maybe the greatest pleasure of getting paid for my writing and having it go out into the world is that my father now believes that there are other people like me, who maybe love the things I love, and laugh at the things I laugh at, and who want to read about these things.

"Son, there's something I've been wanting to share with you."

He said *son*. I stop working and look at him.

"I'm giving up the deaconate."

I can't have heard right. He has spent a decade working toward this position in the Catholic Church. Just last summer he finished earning his master's in divinity and my mother threw one of her swashbuckling parties to congratulate him. Everyone has been looking forward to the sermons that my tough-as-nails, heart-full-of-love father will preach, and no one's looking forward to it more than I am.

"Dad, what're you talking about? It's your dream . . . you've been driving toward it since forever."

He looks off at our snow-covered land. He does this when he needs to concentrate, to get a baseline reading on his life, to remember that he loves this place and his family more than anything else. One time when I was in college, I was watching TV on my parents' couch at two in the morning and my father trudged downstairs in his pajamas and threw on his boots and coat. I asked him where he was going and he said he realized in his sleep that the birch tree out back was sick and he had to go check it out. He wasn't kidding and he wasn't wrong. The tree was sick with some tree disease and over the coming months he did something to save it, though I'll never know exactly what. I think he just stood next to it and talked to it a lot.

"I just can't do it, David," he tells me now on the back deck. "I can't be a deacon. I've learned a lot and I've loved the learning, but my heart won't have it. Catholic deacons are . . . those men are . . . sidelined. I can't serve in a role where I'm . . ." He puts his arm around my shoulders and squeezes. "David," he sighs, "Schicklers just don't like being told what to do."

"All right, Dad."

I go back to fiddling with an inoperable string of lights. There's one faulty bulb somewhere on the chain, and if I don't find it, the whole thing won't work.

FOR MY NEW YEAR'S resolution I decide to start volunteering at the Manhattan Unplanned Pregnancy House. Its literature says that it's a not-for-profit, Protestant faith–based organization that gives counseling and support to women and couples facing unplanned pregnancies. The place will not refer for abortions, but the literature swears up and down that the House isn't a political organization, that it doesn't lobby against the legality of abortion, that it doesn't proselytize Christianity to its clients, and that it uses no scare tactics, no personal appeals, no judgment.

My urge to want to volunteer at M.U.P. House runs deep. Over the years several women I've known have had abortions and have confided to me about it. They've often spoken about the men involved, men who in almost every case weren't there for them after getting them pregnant. I don't presume that I have any great wisdom, and I know that I can't relate to the experiences of pregnant women, and to the credit of the people at M.U.P. House, they never even allow male counselors to try to talk one-on-one with or otherwise counsel their women clients. But they do train male peer counselors to talk to the men in their client couples. And this is where I feel like maybe I can help.

My own longing for women has stirred such fever, fear, and emotion in my own life for so long—and every fraught, naked moment I've ever shared with any girl or woman still lives so close to the surface of my skin and heart—that I know I can relate to the fears of men who feel unsure of their way in intimate relationships. But I can also still always hear the groans my father makes when he hugs and clings to my mother at each day's end, and if there's anything I've learned from those groans, it is that a real man doesn't leave a woman in the lurch. Not that a woman can't be deeply strong on her own if that's what she chooses, but a real man who's facing trouble with a woman doesn't clam up, doesn't bluster or bully or try to dictate, and he doesn't cut and run. I feel very strongly about this, but I know I'll be able to talk about it quietly with other men. I believe that I'll be able to put my yammering Irish mouth to some use by doing so and I believe that I'll be a good, nonjudgmental listener.

And I have one more reason, the deepest possible, for wanting to volunteer at M.U.P. House. For the first time in many years I've asked God for something in my heart. I've asked, *Dear God-if-You're-There: If I do this volunteer work, if I devote myself to it with all that I have, and if, in conversation with other scared men, I try to feel my way through the good but confusing darkness of what it means to try to be one man standing by one woman, will You please give me some small prod, some nudge, some way for me to know that Martha is really my future, my wife? I know now that You'll never talk to me, but can You give me some small prompt so that I'll feel that You're there and that Martha and I can move toward You together?*

I pray this prayer daily. Nothing happens.

I SHOW UP for my first day at M.U.P. House, on the Upper East Side. I meet the two women who run the place, Lillian and Anita. Lillian is in her forties, single, and has long white-blond hair and gives quick smiles. Anita is just a couple years older than I am, married, African-American, with fine cheek-bones and a Sociology PhD. They meet with me in private and ask me many screening questions. They ask if I'm a practicing Christian and I say that I guess that I am and they nod.

"Wait," I say, "what about the clients who come in? It's not a problem for you if they're not Christian, is it? Your literature says 'no judgment.'"

"And we stand by that," Lillian says.

"And you don't proselytize?"

"We don't proselytize."

"Okay."

They approve me for training. I begin the next week. There are thirty hours of instruction over a period of several months. I learn extensive details about adoption and abortion, but the focus is mostly on dialogue do's-and-don'ts. The other future peer counselors and I learn about active listening skills and nonthreatening body language. We also get up to speed on the other services in the city that M.U.P. House works with, from day care and child care centers to doctors to midwives to crisis hotlines. We learn that the House's clientele for the most part are not the poor, but rather working professional women and men.

By July I am trained and ready to work with clients. I'm nervous but hoping to make a difference. My mother has always quietly encouraged me to volunteer or do something charitable and this is the first time I've committed to something where it feels right, where it feels like my life experiences might resonate with others, might help the greater assembly.

Around noon on the day when I'm set to meet with my first male client, I have lunch with Martha at my apartment. She still lives and works in Rochester, and we've been dating long distance for ten months. Right now she's in Manhattan with me for a two-week stay that we've both been looking forward to.

During lunch, though, she seems nervous. We ordered in from It's-a-Wrap, our favorite sandwich and fruit smoothie place, but she isn't eating much.

"What's the matter?" I ask.

After looking at me for a long moment, like she's considering whether to say something, she leans in and kisses my forehead. "It's nothing. Never mind. I just want you to have a good first day."

I thank her. We finish lunch and kiss good-bye and I take a crosstown bus to M.U.P. House. My first client, a man named Greg, is supposed to come in by himself half an hour from now. I get the counseling room ready with bottled water and a fresh Kleenex box in case he gets thirsty or upset. While I'm preparing the room, Anita comes in, closes the door behind her, and sits on the couch.

"David, we need to talk."

"Okay. But can it wait till after my meeting? I could use just a few more minutes to get ready."

"Your client is not coming. Well, he is, but he's coming tomorrow and a different peer counselor will see him."

I sit in a chair opposite her. "What are you talking about?"

"I finally read your book, David. *Kissing in Manhattan*. I bought it and read it."

Normally I would thank her. But she's sitting in the nonthreatening body language position. She's aiming a therapy-ready face at me. For the first time in a long while, I feel the quicksand in my chest, just for a second.

Please, I think toward Anita. *Don't say any more.*

"David, I'm sorry, but . . . well, the things that you wrote in your book . . . they aren't something we can accept in one of our counselors."

I stare at the Kleenex box on the table in front of me, waiting for the rest of the verdict.

"You told us you were a Christian. But the sex in your book . . . the darkness of that main character, that man . . ."

"It's a love story," I say.

"I don't know how you can say that, David. All the swearing, the violence . . ."

My mind careens. I think suddenly of Drake, my old Tapwood student, and his homicidal, killing-spree writing. Then I think, lightning fast, through all of *Kissing in Manhattan*. There's a rich, gun-toting male main character in it who

regularly ties his naked girlfriend to the bedposts in his bedroom and leaves her there while he throws huge parties in the
next room. But he also adores her and he never hurts her physi-
cally and he takes her to the best restaurants in the city and
buys her five-thousand-dollar dresses and dotes on her. And
there's humor and beauty in the book, I think. The girl is naked a lot, but the gun gets fired only once. So, am I Drake?
Maybe I am. Because my writing is about to get me expelled
from something.

"My book," I tell Anita. "It's gritty and weird, but ... it's
real. That's the man's journey."

"We're Christians here, David."

"No judgment." I can barely hear my voice. "What happened to 'no judgment'?"

"We don't judge our clients. But our counselors have to be
in a certain place morally. They have to be completely above
reproach."

I think of my dad in my Columbia days, how he hated my
thesis novel, how offensive he found it. Then I look out the
counseling room window at Manhattan, at the sweet, venal,
fucked-up city that I love. I know only one way to write about
it and that is to tell the truth.

"I'm worried for you, David," Anita says. "Reading
your book, I feel like ... like your heart is full of sin. Choked
with it."

"I see." I'm still unable to meet her eyes.

"I'm worried for your *soul*, David."

"I see."

She puts a hand on my shoulder. "Don't worry, we won't leave you alone to deal with this. If you need to cry, go on, let it out. God forgives even the most stubborn sins. I can recommend you to so many different kinds of counseling—"

I jump to my feet. "I'll be right back. I need the bathroom."

I stride out of the counseling room, out of M.U.P. House.

Fuck them, I think.

I am livid and shaken and will never go back. With my mind spinning, I hurry along East 84th Street and into Central Park. I go to the bridle path around the reservoir where I often run, and I duck under the overhanging branches of my favorite tree, the one I always stretch under. I stand motionless under the canopy of branches and stare out at the reservoir water.

Fuck, fuck, fuck, I think.

My teeth are clenched and I try to relax. Runners trot past on the reservoir path, many of them good-looking girls.

The thought comes that this is the perfect place for me, skulking under a tree, spying out at the trim, sexy legs of young women runners. This is the perfect dark place for a pervert, a deviant apostate who's just been told that he has no business ever trying to help other people, or ever voicing publicly—on the pages of a book, in a counseling room, anywhere—the things that he thinks are beautiful, the things that he thinks are art or salvation. There is nothing priestly about this cretin. He is misguided, a deceiver, a twister of thoughts, words, and images, a man who believes he's taking part in grace when in fact he's a *dis*grace, and a disseminator of disgrace.

Fuck them, I think. *Fuck them all, fuck M.U.P. House, fuck all Christian churches and dogmas, and most of all, fuck You, God, or Lack-of-God, or Whoever the Fuck You Are. Fuck You for the long con that You've been all my life, fuck You for always trying to sucker me back toward You, for making me think that there's a purpose or a place for me, at M.U.P. House or anywhere else, really. And most especially, Fuck Your Silence, which is all You ever give me or any of us. Fuck You, I am cashing out of this one-sided conversation for good. I will do fine on my own, thanks. I will stand apart and alone.*

I stay under the tree. I stand fuming, ashamed, apart and alone.

AROUND SIX I go back to my apartment. I have to tell Martha what happened at M.U.P. House, and that will make me frustrated and sad and furious all over again. It will probably also make me snappish and unpleasant to be around.

When I come in, Martha is sitting in the apartment corner in my brown-leather buster chair. She sits with her arms wrapped around her knees, looking anxious.

"I'm sorry I didn't call," I say.

She shakes her head and waves off my words. But she still looks worried, very worried, and suddenly my shitty day and my agenda of debriefing it seem moot. I sit on the ottoman beside her.

"Hey. What's the matter?"

She shakes her head again. Sometimes she'll do this many times before I can coax words out of her.

She says, "I want to tell you something, and I'm not sure I should. I've wanted to tell you for months, but I'm afraid to."

The quicksand tugs one more time. Martha has already read my book, so I know it won't be about that. *Another man*, I think. *A man back home.*

"Just tell me."

She looks down at her lap. "You have to remember," she says, "that I don't go to church much. Hardly ever."

"I don't care that you don't."

"That's not what I mean. I mean, I don't know all about that stuff like you seem to."

I want to protest again, but I keep my mouth shut.

"The night we met," she says. "You know I don't like meeting new people . . . introducing myself."

This is true. When she came to Thanksgiving at my parents' house, she hid behind doors or tall furniture to avoid greeting relative after relative of mine, and then she walked around clenching my hand in hers, her nails digging into my palm.

"I never would've introduced myself to you at your reading, except for what happened."

I wait.

She scrunches down in the buster chair. "Listen, I'm not a freak. I'm not a wack job."

I say that I know that. I ask her just to tell me.

"I was in the audience, fooling with my cell phone, waiting for the reading to start. Then you came out onstage. And the second that you did and I saw you . . . I don't know how to say it . . . a Voice spoke to me. I heard it in my head and . . . I don't know, my soul. I can't explain. It was strong, like overwhelming, and . . . it came from outside of me . . . and it said, *This is the man you'll spend the rest of your life with.*"

I gaze at her.

Her eyes widen with worry. "Don't freak out! It was just one quick thing I heard and—listen, maybe it wasn't even real."

I can hear all the world's naysayers agreeing. *It wasn't real, David. There was no Voice. Love is a chemical thing. It's Darwinian, that's all.* Well, fuck the naysayers.

Martha waves her hands before her, as if to clear the air. "You're freaking out! I knew it."

It's late in the day, but there's still good sun coming in my windows. And everything inside me is getting sucked out through a point in the center of the top of me. Everything except for the future.

Thank You, Lord, I think. *Thank You, thank You, thank You forever.*

"Forget it," Martha pleads. "I shouldn't have said anything. I never should've told you."

I know a guy who knows a guy who knows a diamond jeweler.

"I just had to say it once," Martha tells me. "Why are you smiling like that? Look, it probably wasn't real. Don't be afraid."

"I'm not," I say. "I'm not afraid."

Chapter Sixteen

I'M FORTY YEARS OLD, sitting alone in the pew at morning Mass, listening to the priest deliver his homily. I don't know this priest, not even his name. He is a stranger to me. I'm in Sacred Heart Cathedral, the main seat of the Catholic Diocese of Rochester.

It is late May and this is Pentecost Sunday 2009, and I'm trying not to glance too often at the woman a row ahead of me and to my left. She is not my wife, but it's nearly impossible not to look at her. She has come to Mass alone, too. Strawberry blond, probably thirty, she wears a silky pale green summer dress that comes to her knees and is cut low on her full chest. A galaxy of russet and light blond freckles covers her shoulders and her long hair is buckled back all cool and hip on her head with what looks like a silver Chinese throwing star. Galaxy Girl smiles when she sings the hymns. She doesn't have a classically beautiful face, but, taken together, her singing smile, her freckles, and her badass throwing star are a funky ensemble. I get a fleeting image in my head of her playing guitar in a coffeehouse and singing Liz Phair's "Perfect World" and nailing it. Then I get a fleeting image of me totally nailing *her*, so I look away again, up at the priest, and I try to hear his words.

My wife, Martha, and our two children are at home. Martha and I lived in Manhattan for six years and then, after we had our first child, a son, we moved back upstate here to be near our families. I'm a full-time screenwriter now and I commute to Manhattan and Los Angeles for work.

Today, Pentecost, is my favorite day of the church year. It commemorates the morning when the Holy Spirit supposedly first came down on the apostles and appeared like licks of flame over their heads and made them speak in every foreign and marvelous tongue imaginable, so that all those in Jerusalem could understand the apostles as they testified about the wonders of God. The apostles that morning allegedly spoke with such wild, leaping force that the crowd thought that they were drunk even though they weren't. So Pentecost is about upbeat wildness. It is about having the guts to say publicly whatever wild truth God put in your heart for you to ponder and then shout about.

The priest's sermon ends. Ushers come down the aisles with collection plates. Galaxy Girl has a sealed Sacred Heart collection envelope and she puts it in the usher's plate. This means that she's a registered member of the Sacred Heart community. When the usher comes to me, I put cash in the plate. I have no donation envelope to seal because I'm not a registered member of this or any parish.

This is what I've come to be: an itinerant, under-the-radar believer who on different Sundays attends Mass at different Catholic churches here or in other cities if I'm traveling. My reluctance to register at a parish runs deep. The Gospels and Mass are vital to me—no matter how many times in life I've pretended otherwise—but I remain as anonymous as I can in my faith. My failure to embrace any one community may cost me dearly some day when I or my family direly need community, but for now I'm a floater, because I worry that the politics and trivialities of life in any one parish might kill God's mystical wonder for me. Coffee and doughnuts and bright nifty chatter after church can still make me uneasy, just like the bright nifty Easter colors used to, the pinks and lavenders. I just can't picture Christ on the Cross, seconds from death, saying, "Oh, crap! I forgot to tell them about Bingo! And Friday-night fish frys!" I still need God to be dire, universal, literally awesome, clobberingly true. This is surely the writer in me, craving drama, needing to strip each character—even myself—down to his or her most elemental motivations.

Martha and I have had our children baptized, and sometimes all four of us come to Mass. But more often, at least lately, I come alone and sit alone and I close my eyes as they're closed now. Alone in this dark, mature solitude, I try as I always have to hear and know God. I may never hear His Voice

as Martha once did—or at least as she and I believe she once
did—but I catch what seem to be whispers of Him in phrases
from Scripture or from the Mass:

In Him we live and move and have our being . . .
I am not worthy to receive You, but only say
the word and I shall be healed . . .

Shakespeare could have written these words: Shakespeare
or some lover, speaking to or about his or her beloved. These
words are alive to me. They and Mass are a poem to me, a poem
about death, and the death of death, and second chances, and
glory. I eat and drink this poem each week and try to join myself to it and be sustained by it.

So I have come to love Sunday morning Mass—I no longer
need to go at night—but there's a chance that the other reason
I don't register officially at any church is my understanding
that, as a writer, I'll never be a Sunday-morning kind of guy.
For whatever reasons, I am good at writing only about Saturday night things, about guns and screwing and liquor and mur-
der and laughter and desperate kissing. When the fiery tongue
of inspiration comes to me, it is a tongue that wants to taste
that galaxy of freckles on the shoulder of that woman in the
next pew, or it's the tongue of a gangster cursing some rival,
promising some bloodbath. It is always a foreign and marvelous tongue, and I try to hear the wild truth in it and write that.

Then at Mass I pray about it. Like right now, even as the priest
blesses the host, I keep my eyes closed and my thoughts race:

Dear Lord, I pray, *help me to love You and Martha and
our children with all that I am. Help me where I can to
help others as You did. But when I'm writing stories,
Lord, please help me to forget all about You, at least consciously. Because if there is one thing that Christian rock
and roll, and various fundamentalisms, and my writing
have taught me, Lord, it is that music and books and
movies that are consciously about You usually suck. They
are forced and cloying and they rise from a fear that if
Your name isn't on our lips at every second, we're doomed.
And I don't buy that we're doomed in that way. I don't
buy that I need to quote the Bible chapter and verse to be
saved, or that every word of Scripture is literally true. I
don't buy that the only thing that You ever want to hear us
say is "God is great" over and over, and I don't buy that
You gave Galaxy Girl her incredible body just so that she
could hide it under a shroud every time she walks outside.
I think You trust us and our imaginations more than
that, Lord, and I think You're cool with Saturday night
things, and so I'm going to trust You back.*

*I'm going to adore my wife and children, and eat the
poem that is Mass, and look at slinky Galaxy Girls, and
sprint through Cobbs Hill Park while listening to that*

song "Flathead" by The Fratellis on my iPod. Or maybe to "A Gentle Sound" by The Railway Children. Have You ever run with "A Gentle Sound" ringing in Your ears, Lord? Do You know that guitar solo? And do You ever splurge, Lord, on wine You can't really afford, and have You tasted Bass ale? Do You help the brewers brew it? And have You ever watched The Office? *Have You seen the final Christmas Special of that show? Did it make You weep, like it made me weep? I hope that it did.*

I'm going to keep going on this path—loving what You've given me to love, writing my Saturday night things—and I'll trust that You'll let there be a drop of grace in all of it. Amen, Lord, Amen.

TEN HOURS LATER, it is a clear-sky evening. I'm sitting in the grass near the tenth-hole tee of Black Creek Country Club, in the spot where Scott Barella and I used to eat our Snickers bars and drink our Sunkist sodas.

Sitting beside me in the grass is my three-year-old son, Luke. He is my and Martha's elder child, and we also have a one-year-old baby girl, Cora. Martha is over at the pool with my mother, where they're dipping Cora into the water to get her to make her happy squeals.

Luke is a blond, blue-eyed, curious little fellow. He loves

to hold my hand and gaze at things with me, so we're current-
ly holding hands and gazing out at the fairways and sky-
scraper pine trees of the Black Creek golf course. I know what
time it is in this place just by the coolness of the air on my skin.

"Daddy, where's us again?"

"Black Creek Country Club. Daddy grew up here. Grandma
and Grampa Schickler's house is just through those woods."

"I always knew that," he says.

He has a dear, complicated way of speaking English. It is a
manner of communicating that doesn't squarely jibe with the
world. I want it to change, so that all will be well for him in life
and so that he'll move forward smoothly. And I want it never
to change because it is purely his, and he's my son. Every day, I
ask him as many questions as I can, just to hear how he will
magically respond.

"Luke . . ." I squeeze his hand. "I wonder whose love for you
is bigger than a T. rex. Do you know?"

He throws up his hands like I'm an idiot. "Daddy!" he
laughs. "That's easy! You're the one who loves me so huge and
I very always knew that!"

There are golfers teeing off on the eighteenth green, meaning that they're headed vaguely in our direction.

Luke points at them. "Uh-oh. Oh, man. Three guys, right
there."

This means that he's worried that their golf balls are going
to hit us, which isn't a danger. But I pull him onto my lap and

tuck his head under my chin so that he'll feel safe. I pull a granola bar out of my pocket.

"Do you want a snack, buddy?"

He sighs. "Well . . . my mouth is unblocked right now."

He takes the granola bar and bites it and chews. I know that while he's eating, he'll be content, so I choose now to ask him the real question I brought him to this spot to ask. He is just this side of four years old, but I still want to know, because for me it started so young and went so deep.

"Luke, look down there. On the other side of that pond."

I point to the dark path. It is a good ways off from us, but it is a clearly visible dell lined with the same overhanging trees it always has been.

"I see," says Luke.

"Does that place look exciting? Should Luke and Daddy go for a walk down there and check it out?"

He chews and swallows. "Well . . . where's Mommy?"

"At the pool with Cora and Grandma Schickler."

"I always knew that." He is still looking at the path. When I show him something, he looks at it deeply, maybe too deeply, like I always have.

"And where's the orange?" he asks.

Whenever there's a good sunset brewing, like there is tonight, Luke calls it "the orange." I tell him that it's behind us, up the hill, beyond the clubhouse. We saw a peek of it when we were walking over here.

"Daddy," he informs me, "it's not a clubhouse. It's a castle."

"Well, then, the orange is behind us, up the hill, beyond the castle."

He finishes his snack. "I want to go look at the orange."

I look off at the dark path for a moment longer. Luke is not zeroing in on it after all. He's not seeing what I always saw. Good for him. I want him to know God and contemplation and love, but I'm hoping it might come to him more calmly than it did to me. I look at him now and I think, *Have adventures, son. Have adventures, but take it easy on yourself. Don't get mono, if you can help it. Don't kick your way into a messed-up leg. Talk to the Lord from your heart and listen for Him but talk and listen to girls, too. Don't choke out any sexually masochistic hotel concierges no matter how much they beg you. Dance your ass off! And never, never think that there's only one way to be holy, only one way for God to love you, or only one path for you to His heaven.*

Luke points at the golfers and says, "Oh, man, Daddy. Three guys are coming. I want to go look at the orange, please and thank you."

"All right, buddy."

I ask him if he'd like to ride on my shoulders. He sighs and thinks it through.

"I very always want to."

I give him a kiss on top of his head. Then I stand and swing him up onto my shoulders and we walk up the hill, beyond the castle, to go look at the orange.

Acknowledgments

If I could, I'd gather these people for a night and pour them wine and thank them for making this book—and my life—so much better.

My parents, Jack and Peggy Schickler, have taught and still teach me joy, patience, and a hundred other graces. Dad and Mom: I love you and am so grateful for your endless, unconditional support. Martha, Luke, Cora, and I are blessed to have you.

My sisters, Anne Marie, Pamela, and Jeanne, make me laugh and always have the back of their freaky writer brother. Thank you for everything except those leotards.

Thank you to my literary agent and friend, Jennifer Carlson, for believing in this book and in me. All of her colleagues at Dunow, Carlson & Lerner have been wonderfully helpful, too. Thank you to my editor, Jake Morrissey, and to Geoff Kloske and everyone at Riverhead for giving *The Dark Path* a home. Ali Cardia, Jynne Martin, Claire McGinnis, and

Darren Ranck at Riverhead have also been amazing for their editing, publicity, and overall enthusiasm.

The four friends who stood up for me at my wedding—Cliff Green, John Dolan, Chris Tengi, and Larry Mastrella—remain my best men and I'd march into Mordor for them. Special thanks to John Dolan for all the Room Time and Basement Time with Luke and Cora. You are their second father.

Alyssa Barrett read all the early drafts and offered discerning encouragement. Thank you, Alyssa, and health and wealth to you and the farmer.

Thank you to Kate Christensen, Darren Strauss, Jonathan Tropper, and Mishna Wolff for the blurbs. Everyone go read their books right now.

In Rochester: thank you to Bob and Alice DeLaCroix, Bob Bradley, Todd Stewart, McQuaid Jesuit, Eric and Rory and the crew at Bruegger's, Joyce at HAI, Tiffany Reynolds, Karey Schmergel, Cassie Shafer, all the Edds, Schicklers, Compisis, and Moszaks, Saint Joseph's, Joe Nicholas, Julie Black, and Mike and Sarah Milano.

In New York: thank you to Dan and Miranda Milledge, Margo Lipschultz, Court Harson, and Ed Nawotka.

In Los Angeles: thank you to Alan Ball, Peter MacDissi, Christina Jokanovich, Kary Antholis and Scott Nemes and everyone at Cinemax for *Banshee*, Shari Smiley, Jim Garavente, David Matlof, Lee Stollman, Ellen Goldsmith-Vein, Lindsey Williams, and my two wonderful agents at CAA, David Kopple and Tiffany Ward.

Marcy Ulrich is my cousin and dear friend and I am grateful to her, Marc, Quinlan, and Griffin for the untiring support.

Thank you to all the Jesuit priests, late and thriving, who have shaped my life and faith, especially Larry Wroblewski, Frank McNamara, and the Georgetown priest identified here as Michael Prince.

I gave these people aliases in the book and I'll thank them as such for their privacy: I'm grateful to Graham, Mason, Daniel, and Austin for their friendship from Georgetown till now . . . to Daphne Lowell and her father, Clement, without whom I would never have survived the crisis in this story . . . and to Mara Kincannon and her sisters and mother. Mara, I learned love and truth just by knowing you. Thank you.

Jonathan Tropper gave me great advice about this book and cocreated the TV show *Banshee* with me. He is an excellent man, writer, father, and friend.

Thank you to my children, Luke and Cora, for showing me, every day, the face and spirit of God in your smiles and shrieks and laughter.

Finally, to Martha Schickler, my forever bride, beyond time: if I had to go through everything in this book to find you, then God bless all of it. Thank you for being my life.